CLASSIC WARPLANES

McDONNELL DOUGLAS
F/A-18
HORNET

Mike Spick

SMITHMARK

A SALAMANDER BOOK

©Salamander Books Ltd. 1991
129-137 York Way,
London N7 9LG,
United Kingdom.

ISBN 0-8317-1412-3

This edition published in 1991 by
SMITHMARK Publishers, Inc., 112
Madison Avenue, New York, NY 10016.

SMITHMARK Books are available for
bulk purchase for sales promotion and
premium use. For details write or
telephone the Manager of Special Sales,
SMITHMARK Publishers, Inc., 112
Madison Avenue, New York, NY 10016.
(212) 532-6660.

All correspondence concerning the
content of this volume should be
addressed to Salamander Books Ltd.

This book may not be sold outside the
United States of America or Canada.

CREDITS

Editor: Chris Westhorp
Designer: Tony Jones
Color Artwork: ©Salamander Books Ltd.
Three-view, side-view and cutaway
drawings: ©Pilot Press, England
Filmset by: The Old Mill, England
Color separation by Graham Curtis
Repro, England
Printed in Belgium by Proost International
Book Production, Turnhout

AUTHOR

MIKE SPICK is a full time writer on military aviation subjects with a
particular emphasis on tactics. Consultant Editor to Air Forces Monthly,
he also lectures, makes occasional television appearances, and does consultancy work
for a European aerospace company. To date he has written more than 25 books,
including ''Fighter Pilot Tactics'' (Patrick Stephens) and ''The Ace Factor'' (Airlife)
while his many works for Salamander include ''Modern Air Combat'' and ''Modern
Fighting Helicopters'', both with Bill Gunston; ''F-14 Tomcat'', ''F/A-18 Hornet'',
and ''B-1B'' in the Fact File series; plus ''Fighter Combat'' and ''Attack Aircraft''
in the Illustrated Guides, as well as contributing to ''The Battle of Britain''.

CONTENTS

THE ORIGINS of the McDonnell Douglas F/A-18 Hornet stretch back a quarter of a century and lie in the archives of another company under a completely different name. In 1966, the Northrop Corporation began actively to seek a successor to its F-5 light fighter, which at that time was in full production, and which, in its A/B and E/F variants, was in service with many nations around the world. Like the F-5, the new fighter was primarily intended for export, and its design would not be influenced by U.S. Air Force (USAF) requirements.

In formulating such requirements, Europe was selected as a baseline theatre of operations. The threat level was high; therefore there was continual pressure to upgrade and enhance operational capability. Several European air forces already flew the F-5, and these it was hoped would favour a further Northrop product. All were industrialized nations, and would therefore probably welcome participation in a collaborative production programme. Finally, Northrop were prepared to offer the opportunity for its clients to participate in the development of the new fighter, thereby gaining technical expertise for the future. Various tactical aircraft then serving with NATO air forces were due for replacement from the mid-1970s onwards; these were primarily early Northrop F-5As, Lockheed F-104 Starfighters, and Dassault Mirage IIIs; about 3,000 aircraft in all. Realistically, Northrop expected to capture about one third of the market.

The next step was to establish the primary role of the proposed aircraft. Both nations and air forces are run by accountants; politicians are in the main merely figureheads. It is the faceless money men who determine budget allocations, and this means that air forces can never (in peacetime anyway) have exactly what they want, but only what they can afford within a limited budget, the direct result being that an aircraft designed for one mission must inevitably carry out tasks for which it was not designed, and for which it is to a degree unsuitable. The main fighter roles were interception, air superiority, ground attack and reconnaissance, and the first task was to determine which set of mission requirements was most compatible with the others. Parametric studies conducted during the first year established that an aircraft designed for air superiority was less compromised in other missions than an aircraft designed for any of the other three baseline roles. The new aircraft was therefore to be first and foremost an air superiority fighter, its main concession to the interception role being a Mach 2 supersonic capability. The final main task was to establish the threat that it must counter. At the time this was thought to be the Soviet MiG-25 "Foxbat", a designation arbitrarily applied by the West to what was at that time widely expected to be a low-cost air superiority development of the highly-successful MiG-21 "Fishbed". With hindsight we know that the MiG-25 was in fact a brute force interceptor totally unsuited to the air superiority mission. This mistaken but realistic appraisal determined that the new Northrop fighter had to be agile, in order to defeat its opponent in close combat. While it would have been nice to have a beyond visual range (BVR) missile capability, this would have called for a much larger, heavier, and more costly machine which would almost certainly have been beyond the financial pocket of most of Northrop's prospective clients.

Left: The F-5E Tiger II was the baseline aircraft for the next Northrop lightweight fighter for the export market.

THE DESIGN TASK

Fighter design tends to be an evolutionary rather than revolutionary process, and the new Northrop fighter was no exception. The baseline for its development was almost inevitably the F-5E Tiger II.

The original F-5A, called the Freedom Fighter, was designed to offer supersonic fighter performance with a limited ground attack capability, combined with simplicity, reliability, and low acquisition, maintenance and operating costs. Unkindly dubbed the true air *inferiority* fighter, it was subsequently upgraded and enhanced to produce the F-5E Tiger II, a much more potent machine but one which retained the same simple virtues of its predecessor. Its turn rates in the subsonic speed regime, both sustained and instantaneous, were on a par with the agile MiG-21, which at that time was the most important and numerous Soviet fighter. Acceleration and rate of climb were good by the standards of the day, while rate of roll was very high, enabling the small fighter to change direction very quickly. But it was unfashionable in being unable to reach anything approaching Mach 2, and in pitch it was a mite sluggish, but handling was crisp, and altogether it was a formidable opponent in the close combat arena.

Close combat, the scenario for which the new fighter was being primarily designed, calls for many different attributes, one of the most important of which is the ability for rapid manoeuvre. Manoeuvre in turn takes many forms. Firstly, the fighter must be able to turn hard. There are two forms of turning — sustained and instantaneous — and three measures of each. The first measure is g, which is an acceleration measured in terms of multiples of the force of gravity. The second measure is the radius of turn, and the third measure is rate of turn measured in degrees per second. Of these, the third is the most relevant to fighter combat. The number of g that can be pulled varies according to how much lift an aircraft's wings can

History and Development

Above: The hooded appearance of the YF-17, seen here on take-off, inspired the name of Cobra.

generate at a given speed and altitude combination, the structural limit of the airframe, and the physical tolerance of the pilot. The radius of turn is almost entirely a function of speed; at typical combat speeds the advantage in turn radius often lies with the slower aircraft. But the most important parameter is rate of turn, which determines how quickly a fighter can generate "angle off" in a defensive situation, or reduce "angle off" when attacking. Absolute comparisons are not particularly relevant, as rarely does a completely neutral situation arise; normally one aircraft or the other has some sort of advantage at the start of an engagement, which may easily influence the eventual outcome.

Instantaneous turn rate is the hardest turn that the fighter can manage at a given height/speed combination. The angle of attack (AoA) is high in order to achieve the maximum possible lift, and this in turn creates extra drag which slows the fighter

down. Maximum instantaneous turn is therefore continually varying as speed bleeds off.

Sustained turn is the highest rate of turn that the airframe/engine combination can manage at a given height and speed. At high subsonic speed and low altitudes the limit is often structural, but at lower speeds or higher altitudes it is aerodynamically limited by lift or thrust constraints. Outside a narrow speed/altitude band, the only time a pilot reaches maximum sustained turn in combat is fleetingly when he passes through it on his way to, or back from, maximum instantaneous turn.

Second comes transient manoeuvrability. This is how fast the fighter can change direction into a turn, climb or dive (or back out of them), and acceleration, which enables it rapidly to regain speed lost during hard manoeuvring. The important factors here are pitch and roll rates, and acceleration. In many ways, these are equally if not more important than turning ability. The classic example dates from 1942, when the Grumman F4F Wildcat could outmanoeuvre the tight-turning Mitsubishi A6M Zero in the higher combat speed range because its transient performance was

superior, even though the Zero could out-turn it at all speeds and altitudes. The difficult but not impossible task of the designers of the new Northrop fighter was to find a compromise between these aerodynamically conflicting requirements.

PROPOSALS

The first proposal, in 1966, was very similar in concept to the F-5E but featured a high-mounted wing with a modest sweep angle, and small leading-edge root extensions (LERX) in order to maintain the excellent handling characteristics of the Tiger II. The engine inlets were set forward, although this in turn required long inlet ducts.

The function of the LERX was to set up vortices over the upper wing surfaces to scrub it clean of the sluggish boundary layer air, and to exploit the phenomenon of vortex lift at the high AoA certain to be encountered during hard manoeuvring. The following year saw greatly extended LERX,

Below: The YF-17 was Northrop's contender in the USAF lightweight fighter competition, competing against the F-16.

while the inlets were cut back to a position beneath the wing. Wing trailing-edge fillets also appeared at this time, although by the following year these had vanished, while the LERX had been increased in size yet again. Also in 1968, the single fin and rudder assembly had been replaced by twin tail fins canted outward. At high AoA, the single fin would have been completely blanketed by the fuselage; twin fins were an answer to this problem. Then in 1969, the LERX were contoured into the now familiar shape and the twin fins were enlarged and moved forward on the fuselage to a position where, at high AoA, they would not be blanketed by the horizontal tail surfaces. In 1970, the P.530, as Northrop had now designated the project, moved closer to being the definitive article when the fuselage shape was refined and the engine intakes cut right back. Slots were formed in the LERX next to the fuselage to allow sluggish boundary layer air to be sucked away before it could enter the air intakes. The LERX gave a distinctly "hooded" appearance to a mock-up produced at this stage, and the name Cobra was duly adopted.

THE LIGHT FIGHTER

Meanwhile, back at the Pentagon, things were stirring. The world's most capable fighter, the McDonnell Douglas F-4 Phantom II, was being given a hard time over Vietnam by the cheaper and simpler MiG-21. Two new American fighters were under development, namely the Grumman F-14 Tomcat and the McDonnell Douglas F-15 Eagle. Large and enormously expensive, it seemed that force sizes would have to be reduced in order to accomodate them. A Pentagon pressure group, widely known as the "Fighter Mafia", argued that austere fighters and lots of them, would be far

Above: The LWF competition was won by the F-16 Fighting Falcon, seen here in the attack role.

more effective than a relatively small force of big ones, regardless of how capable the latter might be. After a lot of infighting, the USAF issued a request for proposals for a lightweight fighter (LWF). Intended purely as a technology demonstrator, few performance criteria were laid down for the LWF, the main requirement being to demonstrate exceptional manoeuvre and handling capability in the transonic regime. Four companies made submissions. Northrop had seen this coming, and had previously commenced work on a new study, the P.600, which differed from the Cobra only marginally, with a slightly amended wing and horizontal tail planform, and more steeply canted fins. There being no Mach 2 requirement, the P.600 had fixed inlets, allowing reductions in both overall design weight and complexity. At the same time, they had proposed a single-engined variant, the P.610, although this subsequently sank without trace. The P.600 formed the

basis for the LWF submission, and on 13 April 1972, contracts were placed with Northrop and General Dynamics to build and fly two prototypes for evaluation. Because at this stage no USAF requirement was to be assumed, this had the effect of putting the P.530 on the backburner, as there was little point in funding a costly private venture which could do little more than parallel work on the LWF, although negotiations with two potential lead customers, Holland and Norway, continued for some time.

For the purposes of the LWF competition, the P.600 was given the USAF designation of YF-17, and the first of the two prototypes was rolled out on 4 April 1974, taking to the air for the first time on 9 June of that same year. About 4ft (1.22m) longer than the P.530, the main external difference lay in the all-moving horizontal tail surfaces, which featured increases in both span and aspect ratio and which were swept more sharply. The YF-17s opponent in the LWF competition was the General Dynamics YF-16, a slightly smaller single-engined aircraft.

History and Development

Even as the first YF-17 was being prepared for its maiden flight, a momentous decision was being taken by the USAF. No matter how capable a fighter truly is, there is a numerical strength level below which an air force would be unable to carry out its assigned tasks. Their chosen future fighter, the large and immensely capable F-15 Eagle, which had not yet entered USAF service, was quite simply unaffordable in the numbers required. The answer was to compromise with a hi/lo mix: adequate numerical strength containing a significant level of high technology. The Eagle would provide the hi-tech element, backed up by a force of austere but affordable fighters optimized for close combat. This had immediate repercussions on the LWF programme; no longer was it to be regarded as just a technology demonstration; the winner was to be developed and bought in large numbers by the USAF.

BIRTH OF THE F/A-18

The LWF was now redesignated the Air Combat Fighter (ACF) and the evaluation programme was rushed through within just a few months. The YF-17 performed extremely creditably, demonstrating a Vmax of Mach 1.95, a combat ceiling of over 50,000ft (15,250m), and a peak load factor of 9.4g. Handling was all that could be desired, there were no adverse departure tendencies, and an AoA of 68deg was attained in manoeuvring flight, which incidentally was far beyond what the opposing YF-16 could reach. But despite this, the award, announced on 13 January 1975, went to General Dynamics' single engined YF-16. At a stroke, all Northrop's work seemed to have gone out of the window, as it now appeared likely that General Dynamics would pick up the export orders which Northrop had

Above: The first FSD F/A-18A shows the revised tailplane and the notched leading edge.

been so confidently expecting for the Cobra.

However, all was not lost. The United States Navy (USN) was in a similar straitened predicament over the cost of the F-14 Tomcat, and at the same time was faced with replacing large numbers of both F-4 Phantom II multi-role fighters and Vought A-7 Corsair II attack aircraft. What the USN really wanted was a new design to fulfil both roles, but for budgetary

reasons Congress dictated that they examine derivatives of both ACF contenders. The Navy acquiesced on condition that both manufacturers teamed with companies experienced in the design of naval aircraft. General Dynamics linked with Ling Temco Vought, while Northrop joined forces with McDonnell Douglas. The Northrop project was numbered P.630.

While in the opinion of the USAF the YF-16 had proved itself the superior dogfighter of the two, USN requirements were rather different. To replace the F-4, the experimental fighter/attack aeroplane (VFAX) would need to carry AIM-7 Sparrow medium-range missiles. These were large and heavy, and on a small machine acted rather like an anchor. A far more capable radar than specified for the ACF would also be needed. For the attack mission, a considerable load of external stores would need to be carried. These requirements dictated that a larger aircraft than either of the two ACF contenders would be needed. There were still other factors. An Air Force fighter spends much of its time over land, where if things go wrong the pilot can eject with a high probability of being recovered, but a Navy fighter inevitably does much of its flying over water, where this is not the case. Two engines give roughly 40 per cent greater safety than one, and this factor was in the YF-17's favour. A carrier fighter is subjected to the continual stresses of catapult launches and arrested landings. Structurally it must be much more rugged than its land-based counterpart. Its wings must fold to reduce the amount of space needed in the confines of the deck park or hangar, and to allow it to fit on the lifts. Finally, a carrier fighter operates in a highly corrosive salt water environment, to which both structure and systems must be resistant.

The USN's decision was stated on

5 May 1975; the YF-17 was to be developed to meet the VFAX requirement. Three main considerations influenced the choice: twin engined safety, demonstrably superior carrier recovery performance, and greater multi-mission potential. The new fighter was to be designated the F/A-18, and later named the Hornet; McDonnell Douglas were nominated as main contractors with Northrop as major subcontractors, the work-split being 60/40. At the same time, Northrop were to develop a land-based variant for the export market called the F-18L; in the event of orders being placed for this the work-split was to be reversed. The F/A-18 would be rather larger and heavier than the YF-17, while the F-18L was to be dimensionally the same as the Navy machine. Because

Above: The Navy attack aircraft to be replaced by the Hornet was the A-7E Corsair II, which had little counter-air capability.

it did not need to be stressed for carrier operations, it would also be considerably lighter.

FULL SCALE DEVELOPMENT

The powerplant of the YF-17 had been developed and uprated to suit the Hornet, a Hughes multi-mode radar was selected, provision was made for two Sparrow missiles to be carried conformally to minimize drag, and extra fuel tankage was squeezed in in order to meet the long-range patrol requirements. The weight increase, caused partly by these modifications and partly by the need to beef up the airframe to withstand carrier launches and landings, caused the wing loading to pass acceptable limits, with a consequent reduction in performance and manoeuvrability. This was cured by increasing the wing area; to keep the aspect ratio pretty much as it was, the span was also increased. Initially a total of 11 Full Scale Development (FSD) aircraft were ordered, and the first flight of the Hornet was set for July 1978. Inevitably there was some slippage, but the first F/A-18, resplendent in blue, white and gold livery,

Below: The Hornet was intended to replace the F-4 Phantom, seen here, in the fleet air defence role, supplementing the Tomcat.

Below: The YF-17 was considered to have more potential than the YF-16 for development into a multi-role carrier fighter.

History and Development

Left: The cant of the vertical tails was adopted to avoid them being blanketed at high AoA.

without the aircraft departing controlled flight. Finally, they acted as compression wedges to lower the Mach number of the air entering the engine, while halving the airflow angle.

At first sight, the wings looked totally unexceptional, having a very modest sweepback of 20deg at the quarter chord position; and a typically Northrop planform with an area of 350ft²(32.52m²). Set in the mid position, they featured variable camber, with leading-edge manoeuvring flaps and plain trailing-edge flaps which, controlled by computer, moved as a function of Mach number and AoA. In this way, the optimum wing profile was achieved. The ailerons, located outboard of the trailing-edge flaps, could also be drooped to give a full trailing-edge flap effect. A missile launch rail was mounted on each wingtip, where it actually helped to reduce drag.

On most fighter aircraft, the wings and tailplane are often similarly shaped, but on the YF-17, this was not the case. The horizontal tail surfaces were swept at a steep angle on the

took off from St. Louis International Airport, Missouri, on 18 November of that year.

The other ten FSD aircraft followed the first into the air at scheduled intervals, and the test programme proceeded apace, revealing a few snags and shortcomings, but nothing that could not be corected. Fifteen years after the first studies commenced, the descendant of the Northrop P.530 Cobra entered USN service, albeit in a guise that was never foreseen at the time. It was the first of many.

As a technology demonstrator, the YF-17 had incorporated many innovations aimed at bestowing agility in

Above: The production aircraft, with most of the slots filled and the leading edge straightened.

close combat, and the majority of these were carried over to become part of the new F/A-18 Hornet. The first, and most obvious such features were the LERX, which extended forward past the cockpit. Acting as giant vortex generators, these increased the Hornet's maximum lift by up to 50 per cent while cutting down induced drag, supersonic trim drag, and buffet. The phenomenon of vortex lift also allowed AoA exceeding 90deg to be attained, albeit at very low airspeeds,

Below: A wide-angle view of an F/A-18 prototype with pre-modified LERX.

leading-edge, and only slightly less at the trailing-edge, with a proportionally large span which exceeded 50 per cent of the wing span. Manufactured in a single slab, the horizontal tail surfaces moved together for movement in the pitching plane, or differentially to provide roll control at supersonic speeds. The outward-canted vertical tail surfaces were fixed, with a movable rudder set low to the rear. The mid-fuselage location was chosen to avoid blanketing by the horizontal tail surfaces at high AoA, with the outward cant chosen to avoid the possibility of biplane interference at low forward speeds. The final moving control surface was the speed brake, located on the rear upper fuselage.

Ailerons, flaps, rudders, and horizontal tail surfaces were all controlled by quadruplex fly-by-wire (FBW), in which if one of the four channels goes down, the other three "outvote" it. The FBW system used on the YF-17 could even survive with two of the four channels out, provided that the other two agreed. Manual control was provided to the horizontal tails as an emergency "get you home" backup. With FBW, the pilot's control inputs are converted into electrical signals, which are then run through the computer. The electrons then decide the control surface movements to be made.

THE ENGINE

In the early development stages, there were two possible choices of engine for the YF-17. Both the General Electric GE-15 and the Turbo Union RB.199 were about the right size, weight and power. While it is now widely accepted that the RB.199 was not really suitable for an agile fighter, being optimized for range and endurance rather than instant reaction to throttle demand, this was not as obvious in 1970, when the most demanding regime for

Above: Hornet No 1 after four years of test flights, carrying AIM-7 Sparows semi-conformally on the intake ducts.

fighters was thought to be full power running for extended periods, rather than continual cycles from full throttle to flight idle and back. The RB.199 was a complex, three-spool engine, and its potential appeal to European users was the main reason for its being considered. However, once the USAF-funded LWF programme was initiated, the American engine became the only realistic choice.

Developed specifically for the Northrop fighter, the GE-15 was a small, two-spool turbofan engine with a bypass ratio so low as to cause it to be dubbed a "leaky turbojet". With development funding from the USAF, it was redesignated the YJ101. The developed J101 was made up of seven major modules for ease of maintenance, and was rated at 9,000lb (40kN) static thrust at full military power, and 14,800lb (66kN) using afterburner. While this rating should

have given the YF-17 an unsurpassed thrust/weight ratio, the ACF evaluation had to be flown using early (and lower rated) development engines, whereas its YF-16 rival used the much larger F100 turbofan previously developed for the F-15. The twelve-petal nozzles were variable, and with no Mach 2 speed requirement, simple fixed inlets were adopted. Their rearward underwing location, small size, and curved ducts helped to reduce radar reflectivity from the face of the engine air compressor, a useful stealth measure, although it was doubtful whether this was intended.

The YF-17 cockpit was laid out in an orthodox manner with the usual dial instruments, a gunsight head-up display (HUD), and a cathode ray tube (CRT) display for the basic Rockwell ranging radar. The Stencel Aero 3C ejection seat was raked at an angle of 18deg, and a one-piece bubble canopy with a single-piece curved windshield gave an excellent view from the "office".

Unlike the P.530 Cobra, which was intended for rough-field operations,

History and Development

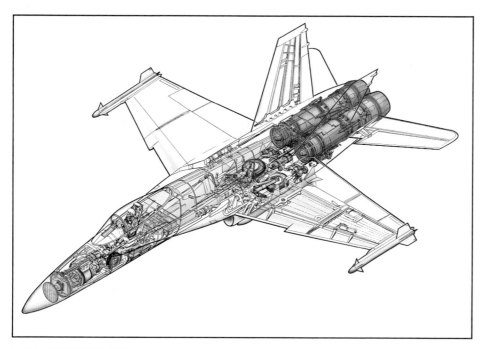

the single-wheel main and nose landing gears of the YF-17 were designed for hard surface use only, which allowed a weight saving.

Turning the lightweight YF-17 air combat fighter into the F/A-18 medium-weight multi-role aircraft suitable for carrier operations was a major task, as evidenced by the fact that whereas the gross take-off weight of the YF-17 was just 23,000lb (10,433kg), the maximum take-off weight of the production F/A-18 Hornet would eventually more than double this, reaching 51,900lb (23,540kg). It was obvious that more power would be required, and General Electric scaled up the J101 to meet the need. The result was the F404-GE-400, a slightly larger and heavier engine rated at 10,600lb (47kN) military power and 16,000lb (71kN) with afterburning. The main differences between the F404 and the J101 were a larger fan and a considerably higher bypass ratio. Residual thrust was very low, an important requirement in the confined spaces of a carrier deck, and anti-corrosion materials were used to counter the hostile environment at sea. Accessories were mounted on the aircraft structure to eliminate specifically "left" and "right" handed engines. An auxiliary power unit (APU) was fitted to

Top: Shown here is the internal layout of the radar, black boxes, fuel, engines, and weapons.

Above: The F404-GE-400 augmented turbofan was scaled up from the earlier YJ101.

Below: The F404 was made modular, easing maintenance and repair work.

**Above: "Look, no afterburner",
as a lightly loaded Hornet leaves
the deck of USS Carl Vinson.**

eliminate reliance on external means for engine starting, and to provide power to various sytems prior to engine start-up, thus reducing the "yellow stuff" needed.

The next step was to beef up the airframe to make it capable of withstanding carrier operations. One of the requirements was that the aircraft should be able to withstand sink rates of up to 24ft/sec (7.31m/sec). Considerable structural strengthening was needed to achieve this, with an attendant increase in weight. In particular, the nose and main landing gears had to be made much tougher, especially with the higher weights involved. The revised nose gear had twin wheels, and the main gears were moved aft a tad to give greater stability for handling on a carrier deck in a rough sea. The fighter mission demanded the carriage of large and draggy Sparrow missiles, and to minimize drag it was decided to house them conformally along the outside of the engine intake ducts. This position complicated the retraction of the main gear, which had to fold backwards while turning through 90deg for stowage. Finally, for carrier operations the Hornet needed an arrestor hook, a catapult towbar on

**Right: The retraction path of the
main gear is complicated by the
position of the AIM-7 Sparrows.**

the nose gear, and a hydraulic wing folding mechanism.

Two further USN requirements caused physical increases in size, which at the end of the day made the Hornet some 12 per cent larger than the YF-17. The first was the need for a much more capable radar. The choice fell on the Hughes APG-65, which was arguably the most versatile fighter radar of its day, but this meant that the nose had to be fattened by four inches (10cm) to accomodate the 28in (71cm) antenna. The second was the need for more fuel; some was carried in the wings, the remainder was shoehorned into the increased fuselage cross-section to give an increase of 4,460lb (2,023kg). It must have been tempting to squeeze even more fuel into the LERX, which were so much empty volume, but two factors

prevented it. The weight would have been too far ahead of the centre of gravity, while any leakage would have gone straight into the engine intakes. In the event, a use was found for the port LERX. A retractable access ladder was stowed there, a little rickety (as the author can testify), but yet another feature to reduce the accessories cluttering up a crowded carrier flight deck.

Ground clearance being limited, an oval cross-section fuel tank was developed specifically for the Hornet. In practice it proved unable to stand up to the stresses of repeated deck launches and landings, and was replaced by a standard cylindrical section tank which held slightly more fuel.

Carrier approach characteristics were vital; a low approach speed and a good view over the nose, implying

History and Development

shallow AoA, were essential. The LERX shapes were fine-tuned, and extended even further forward. The wing area was increased by 50ft² (4.65m²) by extending the span and lengthening the chord, while the settings of the leading- and trailing-edge flaps were tweaked to provide more lift at low speeds. The shape of the horizontal tail surfaces was completely altered to give a much reduced span and aspect ratio, while "dogtooth" vortex generators were added to the leading-edges of both wings and horizontal tail surfaces to check spanwise drift of the airflow.

RELIABILITY

Virtually all high-performance fighters have a two-seat trainer version for instructional purposes. Western practice is to make the "two-holer" completely combat capable, and the Hornet is

Above: FSD Hornet No 3, assigned to carrier suitability trials, overflies USS *America* in October 1979.

no exception. The canopy was extended rearwards, with the back seat slightly higher than the front to give the instructor adequate forward visibility. The second seat displaced 600lb (272kg) of fuel, with the result that this model was slightly shorter legged than the single seater. Overall weights were similar, and the extra drag of the larger canopy reduced performance only marginally.

No matter how good a fighter might be, it is only effective when it is in the air. Reliability and maintainability became buzzwords, and considerable effort was devoted to this aspect of the Hornet. The production article was designed to have a flying life of no less than 6,000 hours, including 2,000

catapult launches and the same number of arrested deck landings. This was a third higher than the two aircraft that it was designed to replace. A premium was placed on maintenance, with much of the Hornet's external surface covered with access hatches, while the avionics are virtually all line replaceable units (LRUs) that can be lifted out easily and replaced by one man wearing arctic gloves. The black boxes are situated at chest height, and are stacked one deep. Less than one tenth of the 307 access panels need work stands to reach them. An engine change should take no longer than 20 minutes, and the current record stands at just 12 minutes. The radar slides out on rails for ease of access, and the ejection seat can be changed without the canopy having to be rerigged. The windshield hinges forward to allow easy access to the instrument panel. Built-in test equipment (BITE) checks out all systems, and information on failures can be called up in the cockpit, or read off from an information panel located in the nosewheel bay. Graphite epoxy composite materials, giving advantages in weight, corrosion, fatigue resistance, and sometimes strength, account for 10 per cent of the structural weight and 40 per cent of the surface area.

REFINEMENTS

The transition from YF-17 to F/A-18 Hornet was not achieved without problems; flight trials revealed certain shortcomings, three of them critical. The rate of roll was slower than specified; range and acceleration were less than predicted; while the nosewheel lift-off speed was too high.

It was subsequently found that the slow rate of roll was caused by flexing of the outer wing panel, coupled with slight roll damping caused by the wingtip Sidewinder missile. At transonic speeds, when the aileron was deflected, the outer wing twisted in the opposite direction. The pilot could actually see the leading-edge curling up! This was cured by a combination of fixes: the leading-edge snag introduced by McDonnell Douglas was eliminated; both structure and skinning were beefed up; the ailerons were extended outwards to the wingtips giving an increase in area, differential movement of the trailing-edge flaps, and increasing the differential authority of the horizontal tail surfaces. An added bonus from the larger aileron was a useful decrease in approach speed as the ailerons were drooped with the flaps.

Range and acceleration were adversely affected by higher than predicted drag. Investigations showed that the slots in the LERX were primarily responsible, and these were subsequently filled in. Flight trials demonstrated that this did not have the predicted adverse effect on the airflow entering the intakes, and this became a standard fix. In addition, the radius of the wing leading-edge was increased slightly, and a fairing was placed over the environmental control system efflux to direct it rearwards. While they had only a marginal effect on acceleration, these three items did improve the range, although not as

Below: The first of the two-seat Hornet TF-18s, later F/A-18B, is seen dumping fuel from vents at the top of the fin trailing edge.

much as desired. At a later date, range requirements were relaxed to meet the demonstrated performance figures.

The excessive nosewheel lift-off speed arose from the main gear legs having been relocated aft to give extra stability on a heaving carrier deck. Two measures were taken to correct this: the ''dogtooth'' in the leading-edge of the horizontal tail surfaces was eliminated, and the flight control computer programme was altered so that when the aircraft's weight was on its wheels, the rudders automatically toed in at an angle of 25deg. With the Hornet in forward motion this caused drag well aft which in turn gave a downward moment astern of the axis of rotation, which raised the nose.

In the early stages it had been assumed that two basic Hornet types would be developed; one optimized for the fighter role, the other an attack aircraft. Basically, the only difference

Above: Configured for the attack mission with FLIR and LST/SCAM pods in the Sparrow positions, this Hornet carries four 1,000lb (454kg) Mk84 bombs.

between the two would have been the sensors and attack systems. The multiple modes of the Hughes APG-65 radar soon made it clear that it was possible to optimize a single variant for both missions, albeit at the cost of a very high pilot workload. It then became a relatively simple matter to adapt both conformal Sparrow missile positions to accomodate sensor pods; a laser spot tracker/strike camera pod on the starboard inlet, and a forward looking infra red (FLIR) pod on the port inlet. This conversion, which could be carried out very quickly, was all that was needed to convert the fighter Hornet into one of the best attack articles.

POSSIBLY the most potent Hornet of all would have been the one that never was, the F/A-18L. This was to have been developed in parallel with the naval version by Northrop, as a land-based fighter for export; and in the event of orders being placed, the 60/40 work split with McDonnell Douglas would have been reversed, Northrop becoming the prime contractor for this variant. The two YF-17s were redesignated F-18L for evaluation purposes, but as no orders were received, the type was never built. The reasons for this are not difficult to find. It is notoriously hard to sell an aircraft overseas if the producer nation is not a customer — as Northrop was to rediscover a few years later when marketing the extremely capable F-20 Tigershark. The selection of the F/A-18A for the USN gave an official seal of approval to the carrier fighter, leaving the F/A-18L out in the cold, even though it was offered under a USN endorsed joint foreign sales

master plan. To further exacerbate the situation, the immediate export competitor was the General Dynamics F-16, the aircraft which had won the ACF competition and been adopted by the USAF. In addition, Northrop found themselves competing for sales against the McDonnell Douglas version of their own aircraft! This situation resulted in a lawsuit which Northrop eventually won, but it was a hollow victory. While the Hornet was successfully sold abroad, it was the McDonnell Douglas carrier fighter which won the day, leaving Northrop with two YF-17s, some impressive looking brochures for the F/A-18L, and financial compensation from their partner.

While the F/A-18L was to have been dimensionally identical with its naval

Below: Hornet of VFR-192 returns to USS *Midway* after a practice bombing mission with its sting-type tailhook extended.

sibling, the catapult launch bar, wing folding mechanism, automatic carrier landing system and tailhook with the attendant local strengthening, were all deleted. The heavyweight carrier landing gear was replaced by lighter units stressed for a sink rate of 14ft (4.27m)/sec. Neither did it have integral wing tanks, although these and a land-based tailhook were optional extras. The result was that the Northrop aircraft was significantly lighter than its naval counterpart; by 2,230lb (1,012kg) empty and 3,800lb (1,724kg) at fighter take-off weight with full internal fuel and four missiles. This resulted in a wing loading of 80lb/ft² (391kg/m²) and a thrust loading of 1:1, compared with the 89.5lb/ft² (437kg/m²) and 0.89 of the carrier aircraft, which was naturally reflected in performance and manoeuvrability. Brochure performance figures showed an increase in top speed of 115kt (213km/hr) at altitude, bringing the Vmax up to Mach 2; a 10 per cent improvement in combat ceiling, and a 12 per cent increase in initial climb rate. An altitude of 40,000ft (12,200m) could be reached in less than three minutes. Acceleration, sustained and instantaneous turn rates were all improved proportionately. At 30,000ft (9,150m), the sustained turn rate at Mach 0.9 exceeded 8deg/sec, and 6deg/sec at Mach 1.2. In terms of sheer fighter performance, the F/A-18L looked to be a rather hotter ship than its naval counterpart. Typical long range air defence configuration was either six Sparrows or six Sidewinders, with two 610 US gallon drop tanks on the inboard pylons and one 450 US gallon tank on the centreline station. A certain amount of strengthening was needed to allow the carriage of

Sparrows on the wingtip rails.

Nor was the attack portion of the mission neglected; the F/A-18L was fitted with two extra underwing hardpoints, bringing the total to 11, although the two conformal points were dedicated to sensor pods, and the gross external load rating to 20,000 (9,070kg); an increase of nearly 18 per cent bringing the maximum overload weight to 52,000lb (23,587kg). In the air-to-ground configuration, 16 Mk 82 500lb (227kg) bombs could be carried along with two 610 US gallon tanks.

In addition to the integral wing fuel tanks offered as an optional extra, other optional extras were an inflight refuelling probe (standard on the carrier version), automatic terrain-following radar, and a video recorder for training. But it was all for nothing. Nations looking for a new fighter bought the F-16 or Dassault Mirage 2000, or, where their requirements were particularly stringent, the McDonnell Douglas F/A-18A Hornet was preferred.

RECONNAISSANCE HORNET

Even with a true multi-role type such as the Hornet, other missions outside the original scope are required. One of these is reconnaissance, and it was originally planned to produce a dedicated RF-18 variant. This was to have been a two-seater, but it was soon realized that extensive structural changes would be needed, as well as a revised environmental controls ystem to cool the extra onboard avionics. This was deemed unaffordable, and the next step was to design a reconnaissance pallet which would be interchangeable with the Vulcan cannon at unit level, the entire exchange operation taking about eight hours. The only external sign of the change in equipment was the gun access housing located beneath the nose, which was replaced by a bulged fairing with

Top: The oval shaped drop tanks seen on this USMC Hornet proved unable to take the stresses of arrested carrier landings, and were replaced by circular ones.

Above: A reconnaissance pallet interchangeable with the Vulcan cannon is seen here, with camera and sensor ports visible in the bulge beneath the nose.

camera ports and sensor mountings. Testing began in October 1982, but this, like so many other cheap solutions, failed to meet the specification, and early in 1984, the USN awarded a development contract to McDonnell Douglas for a dedicated reconnaissance Hornet, which, modified from one of the FSD aircraft, first flew on 15 August 1984, designated F/A-18RC. The reconnaissance equipment is housed in an interchangeable pallet which has two stations capable of holding a mix of USN and US Marine Corps (USMC) sensors. This project has been a long time coming to fruition, but in 1990 the USMC began to take delivery of 31 two-seater F/A-18D Hornets, which are wired to take the sensor pack in a modified nose section. When the sensor pack becomes available, which is scheduled for Fiscal Year 1994, this variant will be redesignated F/A-18RC. This ability rounds out the Hornet's strengths very nicely.

Hornet Variants

The original Hornets were designated F/A-18 for the single-seater and TF/A-18 for the two-seat trainer, which, while fully combat capable, was used for pilot conversion training. These designations were later changed to F/A-18A for the single-seater, and F/A-18B for the two-seater. With the exception of the HUD, the rear cockpit displays are identical to those up front, and repeat the same information. While service entry was relatively straightforward, it was not long before trouble loomed. The problem stemmed from the Hornet's high AoA capability, which exceeded that of any other aircraft then flying with the possible exception of the F-14 Tomcat. Vortices from the LERX at high AoA caused unpredicted side force stresses to be exerted on the canted fins, and through them certain fuselage mainframes, which led to structural cracking. Many of the affected aircraft were grounded, and others limited to 25deg AoA (which incidentally is the AoA limit of the F-16), while a "fix" was sought. This initially took the form of

Below: A Canadian pilot straps himself into the cockpit of his CF-18 at the test establishment at Cold Lake air base, Alberta.

McDonnell-Douglas F/A-18C Hornet Cutaway Drawing Key

1 Glassfibre radome
2 Radome open position
3 Planar radar scanner
4 Scanner tracking mechanism
5 Radome hinge point
6 Cannon muzzle aperture
7 Gun gas venting air intakes
8 Flight refuelling probe, extended
9 Cannon barrels
10 Radar module withdrawal rails
11 AN/ALQ-165 transmitting antenna
12 Electro-luminescent formation lighting strip
13 Hughes AN/APG-65 multi-mode radar equipment module
14 AN/ALR-67 receiving antenna
15 Ventral AN/ALQ-165 transmitting antenna
16 Radar beacon antenna
17 Pitot head, port and starboard
18 Angle of attack transmitter
19 Ammunition drum, 570 rounds
20 Cannon and ammunition drum hydraulic drive motor
21 Cannon mounting
22 Refuelling probe actuator
23 Frameless windscreen panel
24 Instrument panel shroud
25 M61A-1 20-mm six barrel rotary cannon
26 Ammunition feed chute
27 Night identification spotlight (CF-18A aircraft only)
28 Cannon bay access panel
29 Gun bay purging air vents
30 Nosewheel doors
31 Ground power socket
32 Nose undercarriage wheel bay
33 Wing root leading-edge extension
34 Front pressure bulkhead
35 Rudder pedals
36 Control column, quadriplex fly-by-wire control system
37 Kaiser multi-function CRT head-down displays
38 Kaiser AN/AVQ-28 head-up display
39 Upward hinged cockpit canopy
40 Pilot's rear view mirrors
41 Canopy open position
42 Ejection seat headrest
43 Starboard side console panel
44 Martin-Baker SJU-5/6 ejection seat
45 Engine throttle levers
46 Port side console panel
47 Cockpit floor level
48 Avionics equipment bay, port and starboard
49 Landing lamp
50 Catapult launch signal lights
51 Hydraulic steering control
52 Catapult launch strop
53 Twin nosewheels, forward retracting
54 Boarding ladder, extended
55 Hydraulic retraction jack
56 Cleveland nose undercarriage leg strut
57 UHF/TACAN aerial
58 Liquid oxygen converter
59 Cabin pressure regulator
60 Underfloor avionics equipment bay
61 Structural space provision for second seat (F/A-18D)
62 Canopy actuator
63 Canopy lock actuator
64 Rear pressure bulkhead
65 Canopy hinge point
66 Rear avionics equipment bays, port and starboard
67 Fuselage centreline pylon
68 Leading-edge extension frame construction
69 Fuselage void fire suppression foam filler
70 Forward fuselage self-sealing bag-type fuel tanks; total internal capacity 1,415 Imp gal (1,700 US gal/6,435 l)
71 Fuselage top longeron
72 AN/ALQ-165 transmitting antennae
73 Starboard wing root leading-edge extension
74 Graphite/epoxy dorsal access panels
75 Starboard position light
76 Fin aerodynamic load alleviating strake
77 Intake ramp bleed air spill duct
78 TACAN aerial
79 Fuel tank access panels
80 Forward aircraft lifting fitting
81 Avionics equipment liquid cooling system head exchanger
82 Air conditioning system ram air intake
83 Boundary layer splitter plate
84 Port position light
85 Intake ramp bleed air holes
86 Port engine intake
87 Intake duct framing
88 Cooling air spill ducts
89 Port load alleviating strake
90 Air conditioning plant
91 Boundary layer spill duct
92 Air conditioning heat exchanger exhaust
93 Leading-edge flap hydraulic motor and drive shaft
94 Wing root bolted attachment joints
95 Centre section self-sealing fuel tanks
96 fuel bay deck
97 Engine bleed air duct to air conditioning system
98 UHF/IFF Data Link antenna
99 Starboard wing root joint
100 Inboard stores pylon
101 Mk 82, 500-lb (227 kg) Snakeye retarded bombs
102 Multiple ejector rack
103 Outboard stores pylon
104 Starboard wing integral fuel tank
105 Wing fold joint
106 Leading-edge flap, down position
107 Flap rotary hinge actuator
108 Ventral navigation light panelling
109 Graphite/epoxy wing skin panelling
110 Starboard navigation light
111 Missile launch rail
112 AIM-9L Sidewinder air-to-air missile
113 Electro luminescent formation lights
114 Wing tip folded position
115 Starboard drooping aileron
116 Aileron hydraulic actuator
117 Wing fold hydraulic actuator
118 Flap vane
119 Single-slotted flap, down position
120 Flap external hinge
121 Flap tandem hydraulic actuator
122 Rear fuselage self-sealing fuel tank
123 Hydraulic reservoirs, port and starboard
124 Starboard engine bay
125 Fin root attachment joint
126 Fin vent tank
127 Tailfin multi-spar construction
128 Rudder hydraulic actuator
129 Radar warning system power amplifier
130 Graphite/epoxy fin skin panels
131 Leading-edge honeycomb core construction
132 Titanium leading edge
133 Glassfibre fin tip fairing
134 Tail position light
135 AN/ALR-67 receiving antenna
136 AN/ALQ-165 low-band transmitting antenna
137 Fuel jettison
138 Starboard rudder
139 Rudder honeycomb core construction
140 Starboard all-moving tailplane
141 Airbrake, open
142 Graphite/epoxy airbrake frame construction
143 Hydraulic jack
144 Airbrake housing
145 Formation lighting strip
146 Fuel venting air intake
147 Anti-collision beacon
148 Port fin tip fairing
149 AN/ALQ-165 high-band transmitting antenna
150 AN/ALQ-67 receiving antenna
151 AN/ALQ-165 antenna
152 Fuel jettison
153 Port rudder
154 Tailplane mounting frame
155 Afterburner ducting
156 Engine bay venting air louvres
157 Afterburner nozzle actuators
158 Nozzle sealing flaps
159 Port all-moving tailplane
160 Port all-moving tailplane
161 Graphite/epoxy tailplane skin panelling
162 Honeycomb core construction
163 Deck arrester hook, lowered
164 Tailplane pivot mounting

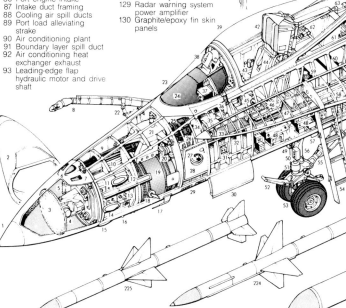
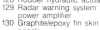

McDonnell Douglas F/A-18 Hornet

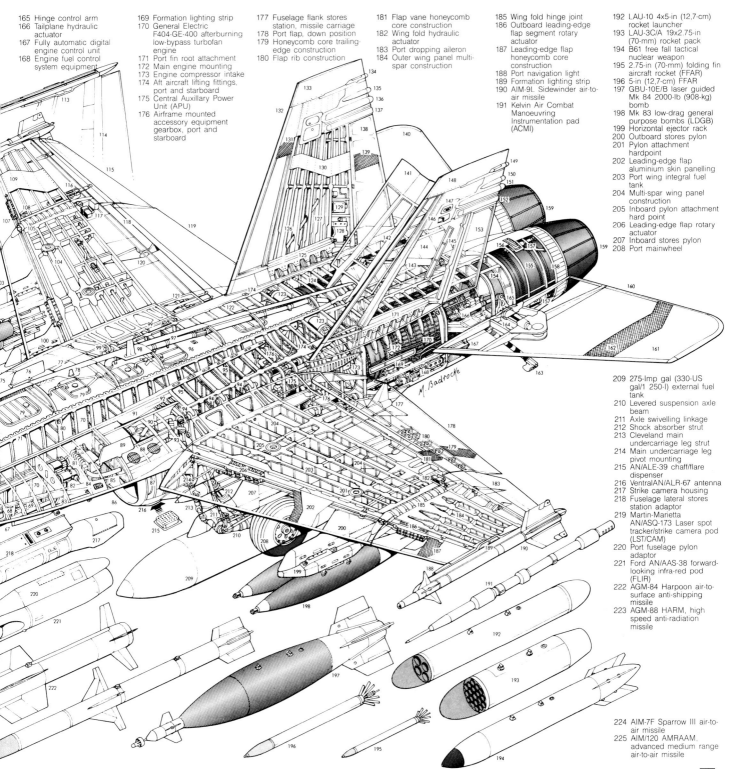

165 Hinge control arm
166 Tailplane hydraulic actuator
167 Fully automatic digital engine control unit
168 Engine fuel control system equipment
169 Formation lighting strip
170 General Electric F404-GE-400 afterburning low-bypass turbofan engine
171 Port fin root attachment
172 Main engine mounting
173 Engine compressor intake
174 Aft aircraft lifting fittings, port and starboard
175 Central Auxillary Power Unit (APU)
176 Airframe mounted accessory equipment gearbox, port and starboard

177 Fuselage flank stores station, missile carriage
178 Port flap, down position
179 Honeycomb core trailing-edge construction
180 Flap rib construction

181 Flap vane honeycomb core construction
182 Wing fold hydraulic actuator
183 Port dropping aileron
184 Outer wing panel multi-spar construction

185 Wing fold hinge joint
186 Outboard leading-edge flap segment rotary actuator
187 Leading-edge flap honeycomb core construction
188 Port navigation light
189 Formation lighting strip
190 AIM-9L Sidewinder air-to-air missile
191 Kelvin Air Combat Manoeuvring Instrumentation pad (ACMI)

192 LAU-10 4x5-in (12,7-cm) rocket launcher
193 LAU-3C/A 19x2.75-in (70-mm) rocket pack
194 B61 free fall tactical nuclear weapon
195 2.75-in (70-mm) folding fin aircraft rocket (FFAR)
196 5-in (12,7-cm) FFAR
197 GBU-10E/B laser guided Mk 84 2000-lb (908-kg) bomb
198 Mk 83 low-drag general purpose bombs (LDGB)
199 Horizontal ejector rack
200 Outboard stores pylon
201 Pylon attachment hardpoint
202 Leading-edge flap aluminium skin panelling
203 Port wing integral fuel tank
204 Multi-spar wing panel construction
205 Inboard pylon attachment hard point
206 Leading-edge flap rotary actuator
207 Inboard stores pylon
208 Port mainwheel

209 275-lmp gal (330-US gal/1 250-l) external fuel tank
210 Levered suspension axle beam
211 Axle swivelling linkage
212 Shock absorber strut
213 Cleveland main undercarriage leg strut
214 Main undercarriage leg pivot mounting
215 AN/ALE-39 chaff/flare dispenser
216 VentralAN/ALR-67 antenna
217 Strike camera housing
218 Fuselage lateral stores station adaptor
219 Martin-Marietta AN/ASQ-173 Laser spot tracker/strike camera pod (LST/CAM)
220 Port fuselage pylon adaptor
221 Ford AN/AAS-38 forward-looking infra-red pod (FLIR)
222 AGM-84 Harpoon air-to-surface anti-shipping missile
223 AGM-88 HARM, high speed anti-radiation missile

224 AIM-7F Sparrow III air-to-air missile
225 AIM/120 AMRAAM, advanced medium range air-to-air missile

M. Badrocke

Hornet Variants

local structural strengthening, but as total Hornet flight time accumulated, this was shown to be inadequate. The final solution takes the form of a small metal strake attached to the rear of the upper surface of each LERX. At high AoA, this modifies the airflow in such a way as to alleviate the forces imposed on the vertical tail surfaces. Though peculiar in appearance, it works!

THE F/A-18C AND D

The next Hornets to enter service were the F/A-18C and D variants. The prototype F/A-18C began flight testing in September 1986, and the first pro-

duction model left the ground just one year later. Externally identical to the earlier models with the exception of a few small excrescences presumably housing aerials, the changes lay entirely in the avionics fit. In the air superiority role it is equipped to carry up to six AIM-120A Advanced Medium-Range Air-to-Air Missiles (AMRAAM) which give the Hornet a multiple target engagement capability for the first time. It has an improved high-speed mission computer with a larger memory, the ALQ-165 advanced self-protection jammer (ASPJ) carried internally, an in-flight incident recording and monitoring system, and

provisions for reconnaissance pods. The original ejection system was replaced by the new ACES seat, giving the pilot a better chance of escape at low level and unusual altitudes. Finally, the C/D variants were equipped to carry the Imaging Infra-Red (IIR) AGM-65F Maverick air-to-ground missile, which has an automatic target acquisition facility allowing first-pass, multiple target attacks.

The next upgrade came quickly, with the C/D models being configured for night and all-weather attack at low level, the prototype of which, a two-seater, first flew on 6 May 1988. The key to the night attack variant is the Hughes AAR-50 Thermal Imaging Navigation Set (TINS), which is carried in addition to the existing Ford Aerospace targeting pod. TINS is a fixed, forward looking infra-red (FLIR) pod-mounted sensor which projects a televisual type image of the area ahead onto a new improved HUD. This enables the pilot to fly, navigate, and locate targets in much the same way as in daylight. Naturally, TINS only gives a relatively small, fixed 20deg field-of-view directly ahead, and unlike the more sophisticated Low-Altitude Navigation and Targeting by Infra-Red at Night (LANTIRN) carried by the F-15 and F-16, it cannot ''look into'' the turn. To overcome this, and to allow him to look around at off-boresight angles, the pilot wears ''Cats Eyes'' night vision goggles(NVG). The cockpit lighting is modified so as not to dazzle the light-sensitive NVGs, which will eventually be replaced by a helmet-mounted sight.

The system has certain advantages over terrain-following radar, in that it is a passive system, with no emissions to betray its presence. A problem encountered in the early days was that the image projected onto the HUD did not quite match the real world view

---

SPECIFICATION

F/A-18C Hornet

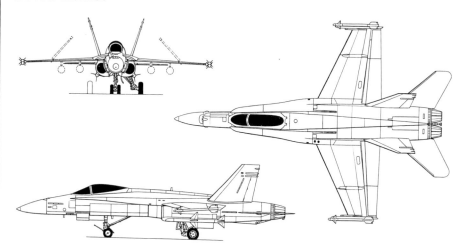

Dimensions
Length: 56ft (17.07m)
Height: 15ft 3½in (4.66m)
Wing span: 37ft 6in (11.43m)
Gross wing area: 400 sq ft (37.16m²)

Weights
Empty: 23,000lb (10,433kg)
Normal take-off weight: 36,970lb (16,769kg)
Maximum take-off weight: 51,900lb (23,540kg)
Maximum external weapons load: 17,000lb (7,710kg)

Power
2 x General Electric F404-GE-402 turbofan

Maximum thrust: 16,000lb (71.2kN)
Internal fuel: 10,860lb (4,925kg)
External fuel: 7,000lb (3,137kg)

Performance
Maximum level speed, high-level: Mach 1.7 (1,122mph 1,806km/h)
Maximum level speed, low-level: Mach 1.01 (666mph 1,073km/h)
Combat ceiling: 50,000ft (15,240m)
Combat radius, attack: 575nm (1,065km)
Combat radius, fighter: 405nm (751km)
Unrefuelled ferry range: 2,000nm (3,706km)

that the pilot could see through his "*Cats Eyes*", leading to a double image which could cause confusion at low-level. A software adjustment has since corrected this. A further addition is a digital colour moving-map display, driven by a laser disc on which threat and intelligence information can also be stored.

Although fully combat capable, two-seater Hornets have been traditionally used for pilot training, and in USN service this will continue. Night Attack F/A-18Ds operated by the USMC are a departure in this respect, as a flight officer occupies the rear seat and operates the weapons systems. His control column and throttles have been removed, and two fixed hand controllers installed to drive the weapons systems and the displays. The three HUDs are decoupled, and can be operated independently of what is happening in the other cockpit. This will allow the USMC Hornets to replace the elderly all-weather Grumman A-6E Intruder in all roles except deep strike, for which the ill-fated A-12 Avenger II was being developed before cancellation in early-1991.

A modification kit is provided for aircraft delivered to the USN, allowing the service to fit a control column and throttles in the rear cockpit for training purposes.

Of all the aircraft of its generation, the Hornet is the last to receive a radar update, which speaks volumes for the capability of the original APG-65. An upgrading contract was placed in June 1990 for service entry in 1994. New technology will be incorporated, increasing the speed of data processing by a factor of more than three and signal processing by eight or more, while improving the sensitivity of the receiver. This will give better performance in the face of hostile jamming; improve discrimination in the raid assessment mode; and give much greater resolution for the ground

Above: Tail fin reinforcement and a strake above the LERX can be seen on this brand new F/A-18C.

Below: Cockpit MFDs reflecting on his dark visor enhance the high-tech Hornet pilot image.

Above: Even in the attack mode the Hornet retains Sidewinders on wingtip rails for self-defence.

mapping, while providing capacity for additional modes. No details of other operational modes have been released at the time of writing, but automatic terrain following appears to be a possibility, while it is known that the USMC would like a beacon bombing mode for the night close air support (CAS) mission. The beacon is put in a known location by a forward air controller (FAC) on the ground, and its co-ordinates are passed to the Hornet backseater, together with the distance and bearing of the target from it. The beacon is then detected by the aircraft, which uses it as an offset target marker, allowing a first-pass, precision blind strike to be carried out.

Another area in which the Hornet lags its contemporaries is re-engining. This is also being corrected; from August 1991, new-build Hornets will be powered by the General Electric F404-402 enhanced performance engine, giving up to 20 per cent more thrust at high speeds and high altitudes. Increased mass flow will require a slightly larger intake. The

F404 has still more growth potential, and it is expected that 20,000lb (89kN) static thrust will be reached in the near future.

HORNET 2000

Proposals for advanced Hornets were revealed by McDonnell Douglas in October 1987. The main question posed was what would be needed by the end of the century. However, development inevitably leads to weight growth, with a consequent loss of performance. More power is an obvious need, but extra thrust calls for more fuel. More fuel means extra weight, and often extra volume, which increases drag. Even if the thrust/weight ratio is kept within acceptable limits, wing loading inevitably goes sky high, increasing field performance and reducing turning ability. The problem then becomes, at what point does one

compromise? McDonnell Douglas addressed the problem in four stages.

Proposal I had minimal impact on the airframe. It consisted of an upgraded cockpit, weapon system updates, and increased thrust, all of which could be contained within the existing volume. The benefits were improved situational awareness, transonic and supersonic performance, and greater survivability.

Proposal II was to expand mission flexibility by increasing internal fuel capacity by 2,700lb (1,225kg), the fitting of a growth engine, and wing stiffening to give higher ordnance carriage speeds. An active array radar antenna would more than double target detection range, while its electronic beam steering might allow simultaneous mode operation. Passive missile detection and laser warning gear would also be incorporated.

Proposal III was aimed at restoring manoeuvre and carrier wind over deck requirements previously degraded by the weight increases of the earlier proposals, while increasing the mission

Right: Who needs fighter escort with agility like this, even though laden with bombs?

flexibility still more. Wing loading was to be brought back to par by replacing the stiffened wing with one of greater area, albeit of identical planform, and internal fuel capacity was to be increased by 3,700lb (1,678kg), part housed in the new wing, and part in the fuselage by raising the dorsal area behind the cockpit. Extra avionics growth space would be made available, and the horizontal tail surfaces would be enlarged. An amendment to this, proposal IIIA, was to have stretched the fuselage to accomodate the extra fuel, thus eliminating the extra drag caused by the raised dorsal area in transonic and supersonic flight.

Finally, Proposal IV involved a radical redesign using control configured vehicle (CCV) technology. This consisted of close-coupled canard foreplanes combined with a cranked delta wing cobbled on to the Hornet fuselage. The vertical tail surfaces were given a marked increase in area, and a fuselage plug was inserted. Finally, internal fuel capacity was increased by 3,200lb (1,452kg) more than the baseline aircraft. This configuration, which became known as Hornet 2000, was aimed at providing increased agility, and it was hoped that European nations which at that time were in the early stages of developing the next-generation European Fighter Aircraft (EFA) and the Dassault-Breguet Rafale, might be interested.

So far, there have been no takers. This is not to say that there never will be, and the recent outbreak of peace in Europe might have the effect of shelving some of the more advanced, or more expensive projects currently in the offing, which in turn might just open up a gap in the market. If so, the ''big wing'' Hornet may well emerge as the front runner.

IN ORDER to carry out both the air superiority and ground attack roles with equal facility, the Hornet was given a very advanced avionics fit. At the heart of this was the Hughes APG-65 radar. Hughes had previously built the first mass-produced radar with a track while scan facility; the F-14 Tomcat's AWG-9, which could track up to 24 aerial targets while sorting out the six greatest threats for display and simultaneous attack. This was followed by the APG-63 radar for the F-15 Eagle. This was optimized for the air-to-air role, and while it lacked the multiple attack capability of the AWG-9, it introduced medium pulse

Above: The bubble canopy of the Hornet gives excellent vision through 360deg.

repetition frequency (PRF), which gave better detection and more accurate ranging against low closure rate targets. The APG-65 had to give almost equal capability in the air superiority role while having excellent navigational and surface target performance, and being compact enough to fit in the nose of the Hornet. Its modes are:

AIR-TO-AIR MODES.
Velocity Search is a high PRF mode which is mainly used to detect closing contacts out to about 100nm (185km). It tells the pilot which direction the contact is coming from, and how fast it is approaching, but not how far away it is.

Range While Search uses both high and medium PRFs to detect anything within about 80nm (148km) regardless of aspect, heading, velocity or closure rate. If in this mode a contact comes within weapons range, Single Target Track is automatically cued on the HUD, the pilot then switches to this mode.

Single Target Track (STT) uses two-channel, monopulse angle-tracking which can follow a contact through most manoeuvres without breaking lock, provided that the Hornet pilot can keep his nose within the radar antenna gimbal limits. The aspect, velocity and altitude of the contact are shown on a cockpit display, while steering commands and attack data are displayed on the HUD. When a firing solution has been achieved, a flashing light on the canopy bow illuminates the ''shoot'' caption. This mode provides radar illumination for the Sparrow missiles; when using Sidewinders, the HUD confirms which target the missile seeker head is looking at prior to launch.

Track While Scan (TWS) medium PRF mode used at ranges below 40nm (75km) to track contacts already made while continuing to search for others. It can maintain files on ten different contacts, while displaying the eight greatest threats on the screen. The contact posing the greatest threat also has its aspect, velocity and altitude

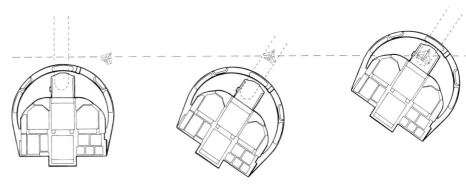

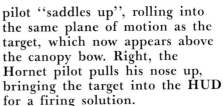

shown. TWS will be the mode used for AIM-120A AMRAAM guidance during simultaneous attacks on multiple targets.

Raid Assessment (RA) is a mode used to sort out individual aircraft flying in close formation, which in other modes produces a single blip on the screen. Effective at ranges up to 30nm (55km), the RA mode expands the area around a single blip to give increased resolution.

Boresight is a mode which utilizes the time-honoured method of pointing the aircraft's nose at an opponent. A very narrow 3.3deg radar beam is aligned with the centreline of the Hornet, which must then manoeuvre to hold the target in it.

Below: The Hughes APG-65 multi-mode radar pulls out on rails for ease of access when servicing is needed.

Above: The vertical acquisition mode projects a 5deg wide beam through an arc between 60deg above and 14deg down, as seen here. At left, VA mode has been selected, with the target high to the right. Centre, the Hornet

Vertical Acquisition scans through an arc 60deg above to 14deg below the Hornet's centreline with a narrow beam only 5deg wide. This mode is used in a turning fight; the Hornet pilot "saddles up" by rolling into the

pilot "saddles up", rolling into the same plane of motion as the target, which now appears above the canopy bow. Right, the Hornet pilot pulls his nose up, bringing the target into the HUD for a firing solution.

same plane of motion as the target, and waits for the radar to lock on. If the target is above the canopy bow, the Hornet pilot must pull to gain angles; while if it is out of sight below the nose, the system will cue a shot when a firing solution has been achieved.

HUD Acquisition scans the 20deg x 20deg field of view through the HUD, giving angles of 10deg on either side, 14deg above and six deg below boresight.

Boresight, Vertical Acquisiton, and HUD Acquisition are all close-combat modes usable at ranges of 500ft (150m) out to 5nm (9km). Target acquisition is automatic once the mode has been selected, and once a firing solution is reached, visual "shoot" cues appear on the cockpit displays, the HUD, and the canopy bow indicator. While the system acquires the target automatically, the pilot retains the option to "step through" to the next target, or the one after, if he so wishes.

Gun Director is the final short-range combat mode. The radar gives data on range, aspect, position and velocity

Avionics and Armament

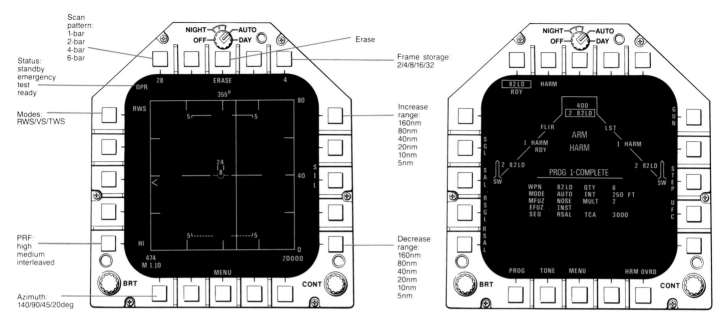

Scan pattern: 1-bar 2-bar 4-bar 6-bar

Status: standby emergency test ready

Modes: RWS/VS/TWS

PRF: high medium interleaved

Azimuth: 140/90/45/20deg

Erase

Frame storage: 2/4/8/16/32

Increase range: 160nm 80nm 40nm 20nm 10nm 5nm

Decrease range: 160nm 80nm 40nm 20nm 10nm 5nm

of the target, which in turn drives the gunsight aiming point, or "pipper", around the HUD, making due allowance for angle-off and lead. This greatly simplifies deflection shooting at high angles-off; the pilot places the "pipper" on the target and triggers off a burst.

AIR-TO-SURFACE MODES

In order to attack a surface target, it is first necessary to find it. While this is not too difficult in clear skies with unlimited visibility, the war does not stop when skies are overcast or night has fallen. Consequently, many of the air-to-surface modes of the APG-65 are devoted to finding the target in adverse weather. The air-to-surface modes are:

Real Beam Ground Mapping Mode produces a crude small-scale map of the terrain ahead, on which prominent features such as river estuaries and lakes can be seen. The radar map picture is automatically adjusted for vertical presentation. To obtain more detail, two supplementary modes are used. These are:

Above Left: A typical example of the Multi-Function Display (MFD) symbology, showing the radar in Range While Search mode to track a target flying slightly higher.

Above Centre Left: The ordnance status (attack configuration), with the AGM-88 HARM selected.

Above Centre Right: Track While Scan mode, as the Hornet moves to the left.

Above Right: An example of the Hornet's horizontal situation and mission data display.

Doppler Beam Sharpening (DBS) Sector Mode, which gives a selected portion of the map magnified to a ratio of 19:1, and **DBS Patch Mode**, which blows up an even smaller area of the map to a magnification ratio of 67:1. **DBS Sector Mode** allows easier identification of areas, while **DBS Patch** permits the detection of relatively small targets such as runways.

Terrain Avoidance Mode presents

two sets of data to the pilot; one is the ground profile along the direction of flight, the other shows obstacles rising above a certain preset altitude along the line of flight. It is then up to the pilot to take avoiding action. When the Hornet is in a nose-down attitude the terrain along the line of flight is displayed, but when it is nose-up the terrain parallel to the ground is depicted.

Precision Velocity Update Mode is used to improve navigational accuracy by feeding velocity data to the ASN-130 inertial navigation system (INS), which has demonstrated an accuracy of 0.5nm (0.93km) per hour. It also provides Doppler inputs to the weapons aiming computer.

Fixed Target Track (FTT) Mode uses two-channel monopulse angle tracking and frequency agility (synthetic aperture) to track fixed targets with a significant radar return. This can be used for direct attack, or to use a radar reflective point as a navigational waypoint or an offset identification feature for a first-pass blind strike.

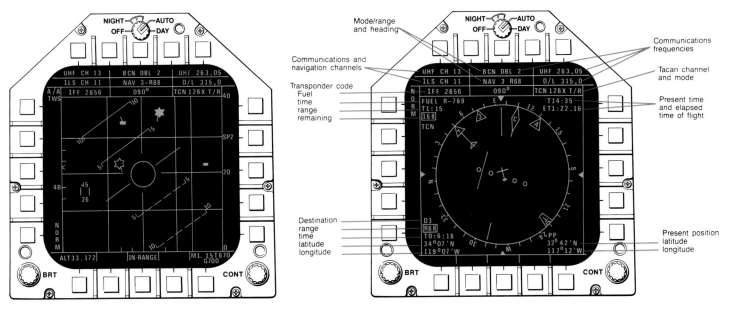

Ground Moving Target Track Mode uses the same synthetic aperture techniques as FTT mode to detect and track moving targets on the ground.

Air-to-Surface Ranging Mode is used to actually deliver the ordnance on target. There are two variations on this theme; when the attack calls for a small depression angle, monopulse angle tracking is used, whereas at large depression angles split-gate range tracking is used. Target acquisition is automatic in this mode, which can also be used to provide ranging data when the target is designated by external means, such as laser or infra-red.

Sea Surface Search Mode is essential for a carrier-based fighter, although as shipping targets move relatively slowly, a tracking capability is not incorporated. To overcome the problems caused by rough seas, the radar first samples the sea state, then automatically establishes a threshold at which the background clutter will be filtered out. The radar then displays only those objects which do not conform to the threshold limit, which are likely to be ships.

When equipped for the attack role, the Hornet carries two sensor pods on the fuselage Sparrow missile stations. These are the Ford Aerospace AAS-38 FLIR, and the Martin Marietta Laser Spot Tracker/Strike Camera (LST/SCAM).

The FLIR provides a modicum of night and adverse weather attack capability by projecting a heat contrast image of the terrain below in conditions too bad for the human eyeball to function. The field-of-view is 12deg x 12deg, and this can be trained at angles between 30deg up and 150deg down, this last figure giving a rearward and downward view. The electrons are programmed to present the image actual size and the right way up, i.e. as the pilot would see it. When something of interest is sighted, the field-of-view can be closed down to 3deg x 3deg, giving a magnification ratio of roughly 4:1, and auto tracking can then be engaged, and used to feed accurate weapons delivery data into the attack system. The head continues to track even after the Hornet has overflown the target, which allows

an instant assessment of the effectiveness of the attack to be made.

The LST/SCAM pod has two functions. Firstly, the LST searches for, acquires and tracks pulse-coded laser energy reflected from a predesignated target. This allows target acquisition from beyond normal visual range even when the Hornet is being thrown about to deceive enemy ground defences, and allows a first-pass blind strike to be made. Secondly, the 35mm panoramic strike camera films the target area throughout the attack sequence to record events, and to see if anything else of interest is in the immediate area.

Space does not permit a full description of the other avionics carried by the Hornet; like all modern fighters it carries the usual fit of black boxes; navigation and communications kit; data link, IFF, RWR etc. The pilot has to fly the aeroplane, navigate, and generally sort out the mass of information with which he is being deluged in order to carry out the mission. The real problem lies in trying to keep the pilot's workload within manageable limits. The cockpit of the

Avionics and Armament

YF-17 was quite ordinary, but it was designed for a fairly simple mission. The multiple missions for which the Hornet was optimized are far from simple, and in the earlier F-4 had demanded a two-man crew. The task then became the classic one of getting a quart into a pint pot; reducing the workload to the point where one man could do a convincing job without the danger of "maxing out". McDonnell Douglas rose to the challenge magnificently, and the Hornet cockpit design, later to be described by Hornet drivers as "like something out of *Star Wars*", can rightly be said to have set totally new standards.

McDonnell Douglas had been fairly innovative in designing the cockpit of the F-15 Eagle, and a lot of their ideas were carried over into the Hornet. The Hornet is a smaller aircraft, but the original 18deg seat angle of the YF-17 has been retained, raising the knee line of the pilot higher, further reducing available space. Compared with the F-15, the Hornet has only about 60 per cent of useable dash and console area, while having more systems to control and display.

The solution adopted was the first "glass" cockpit, with three multi-function displays (MFD) replacing conventional dial or tape instruments, coupled with the Hands On Throttle And Stick (HOTAS) control system pioneered on the Eagle. The MFDs allow the pilot to call up the precise information he wants at any given moment at the touch of a button, while the latter ensures that all functions needed in the time-critical combat regime are readily to hand.

The Hornet cockpit is totally unlike that of any previous fighter, with four main displays, all produced by Kaiser Aerospace. The HUD is the main flight instrument for weapons delivery, navigation and carrier landings. A twin combiner type, it has a 20deg x 20deg field-of-view. Symbolic or alpha-

Above: The cockpit layout means one man can operate with ease. Data is called up on the CRT screens at the touch of a button.

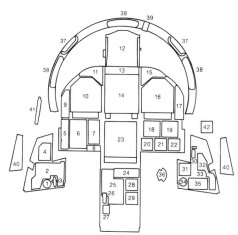

1 Brake pressure indicator
2 Landing hook bypass, launch bar and stores jettison selectors
3 Emergency/parking brake handle
4 Landing gear controls
5 Stores jettison indicators
6 Digital engine monitor display
7 Fuel quantity indicator
8 Course and heading lightplate
9 Master armament panel
10 Master monitor display
11 Left warning panel
12 Head-up display
13 Head-up display camera
14 Up-front control panel
15 Right warning panel
16 Multi-function display
17 IR cooling, map gain and ILS/Deck landing switches
18 Attitude reference indicator
19 Radar warning display
20 Standby airspeed indicator
21 Standby altimeter
22 Vertical speed indicator
23 Horizontal situation display
24 ECM growth space
25 ECM control panel
26 Rudder pedal adjustment
27 Aircraft build-number plate
28 Clock
29 Cabin pressure altimeter
30 Arrester hook control
31 Altitude indicator
32 Landing lightplate
33 Wing fold control
34 Hydraulic pressure indicator
35 Caution light panel
36 Static-pressure source selector
37 Canopy frame handle
38 Mirror
39 Lock/shoot indicator
40 Environmental control system louvre
41 Canopy jettison lever
42 Standby magnetic compass

numeric information is focussed on it at infinity, to allow the pilot to manoeuvre, carry through an attack, or land on a carrier deck, without the need to glance down into the cockpit at a crucial moment. The dashboard is dominated by three 5in (12.7cm) square displays; two set high to left and right, the third low and central. Each consists of a 5in (12.7cm) cathode ray tube (CRT) surrounded by 20 push buttons which select operating modes or computer programmes. Identical units, their functions are interchangeable in the event of one failing.

At top left on the dashboard is the MFD, which is the primary display for radar, attack, and mapping information. It also shows flight information such as speed, altitude, attitude, and weapon status. The Master Monitor Display (MMD) is located at the top right of the instrument panel, and is the main warning, electro-optical and infra-red sensor display. It also gives cautionary and advisory information on aircraft systems, such as a warning if oil or hydraulic pressure has started to drop. The third, central display is the horizontal situation indicator (HSI), a film-projected, coloured moving map which also shows navigation information such as INS waypoint and tactical air navigation (TACAN) steering commands, and attack information such as time and distance to target. It also shows electronic warfare and threat indications.

Located just beneath the HUD, and between the three head-down MFDs, is the control panel for navigation, communications and identification functions. This controls such items as the two ultra-high frequency (UHF) radios, automatic direction finding (ADF), instrument brightness, IFF, TACAN, Data Link, Automatic Carrier Landing System (ACLS), among other things.

A few functions are still done in the

old-fashioned way. Fuel and engine status information is shown on drum counters, while master warning lights flash if anything is going wrong, although in the latter case, details of the malfunction appear at once in a corner of either the MFD or the MMD. For emergency back-up, a few standby instruments are located at the bottom right of the dash. They consist of pneumatically driven altimeter, airspeed and rate-of-descent indicators, plus a gyroscopic attitude indicator. In orthodox fighters, the pilot has an awful lot of things to look at and monitor, but the "glass" cockpit represents a credible attempt to put the essentials all in one place in an easily understood format.

In addition to absorbing information from sensors and flight instruments, a fighter pilot has to be

Below: Taking its lead from the F-15, the F/A-18 has combined the throttle with a control stick to enable the pilot to cope with the complex range of weapons and sensors. The concept is HOTAS, or hands on throttle and stick. In the fast modern fighter environment this ability to offer a split-second more may be vital.

able to act on it. The classic case is combat, when he dare not take his eyes off a distant fleeting dot in the sky, or a tank three miles (5km) distant, for fear of losing it, and yet at the same time he needs to change radar modes, or arm the right sequence of weapons. In an earlier generation of fighters these tasks might take several switch movements.

Above: Pilot's eye view astern as a Hornet climbs away from its carrier base. This picture shows how well the dangerous blind spots have been reduced.

Opportunities could all too easily be missed through fumbling with a gloved hand made nervous by the tension of battle. This problem had been addressed by McDonnell Douglas in the cockpit design of their F-15 fighter, and the answer had been the HOTAS concept, in which every switch needed by the pilot in a combat situation was placed on the throttle levers or the control column, where they were immediately to hand. The naval pilot has an almost equally demanding situation arising at much more frequent intervals, carrier deck landings. HOTAS was therefore incorporated in the Hornet from the outset and has made it one of the best aircraft to handle.

A total of 17 switches make up the HOTAS system of the Hornet, 10 on the twin throttle levers and the remaining seven on the control column.

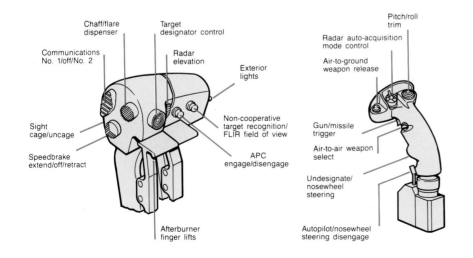

Avionics and Armament

Above: A far from comprehensive view of ordnance cleared for carriage by the F/A-18 Hornet.

While this calls for a high level of manual dexterity to operate, not only are the 17 switches under hand, but they are all identifiable by touch.

The switches on the control column are: the Air-to-Air Weapon Selector, the Gun/Missile Trigger, the Air-to-Ground Weapon Release button, the Radar Auto-Acquisition Control, all of which are concerned with weapons usage; Pitch/Roll Trim Control, Undesignate/Nosewheel Steering, and the Autopilot/Nosewheel Steering Disengage. On the throttle levers are mounted the Target Designator Control, Radar Elevation Control, Missile Sight Cage/Uncage, Speedbrake, Non-Cooperative Target Recognition/FLIR Field-of-View Control, and the Chaff/Flare Dispenser, all of which are likely to be needed in combat, plus the Approach Power Compensator used in deck landings, radio communications, and anti-collision lights. Two finger lifts allow the throttles to be advanced through the detents into the after-burning regime. For many of these controls, the name explains the function, but the complex working of

the other modes needs a more detailed explanation.

The **Air-to-Air Weapon Selector (AAWS)** has three positions, for Sparrow and Sidewinder missiles, and guns. The radar automatically sets itself to the parameters of the weapon chosen, taking range, azimuth, and elevation into account. When Sparrow is selected, the radar enters RWS mode out to a maximum distance of 80nm (148km), with a wide but shallow scan pattern, while for Sidewinder maximum range reduces to 20nm (37km) with a narrower but deeper scan pattern, while if the gun is selected the maximum range becomes 5nm (9km), with an even narrower and deeper scan pattern. In practice, the AAWS provides an easy way for the Hornet driver to change his search pattern, simply by altering the weapon selected. An anti-finger trouble aid is a check of which weapon is selected, given on the MFD.

The **Radar Auto-Acquisition Control** also has three switch positions, corresponding to the three close-combat radar modes of Boresight, HUD Acquisition, and Vertical Acquisition. In all these modes, lock-on is automatic, and "shoot" cues appear on both HUD and MFD when a firing position is reached.

Pitch/Roll Trim is used to balance the Hornet in unusual flight regimes, such as a steep dive or climb, or when an assymetric load is carried, such as when some of the external stores have been expended.

The **Target Designator Control (TDC)** is a force transducer which moves the designator brackets on the displays to select a specific radar mode, or by slewing it to cover a target symbol on the HUD, a press of the button locks onto it. When FLIR and LST/SCAM are carried, the TDC can also be used to modify the line-of-sight of their sensors.

The **Radar Elevation Control** selects either look-up, look-level, or look-down, by the radar, and is primarily used in the velocity search and range-while-search modes, although it can also be used with TWS.

The **Missile Sight Cage/Uncage** switch controls the seeker heads of the Sidewinders. When caged, (or engaged), it automatically slaves the IR seeker heads to the line of sight of the radar, allowing rapid acquisition of the target prior to launch.

FIREPOWER

As would be expected of a dedicated multi-role fighter, the Hornet is cleared to carry a wide variety of weaponry. It has a total of nine hard-points, giving a theoretical maximum external stores load of 17,000lb

(7.711kg). This is theoretical in as much as it is the total of the maximum load ratings of the various hardpoints. In practice, it is difficult to find loads which match the maximum of each 'point, and the result is that the maximum practical load is somewhat less than the book figure.

The air-to-air weaponry carried by the Hornet consists of a 20mm cannon, and a combination of AIM-7 Sparrow and AIM-9 Sidewinders. In the early-1990s, Sparrow will be replaced by AIM-120A AMRAAM.

The cannon is the tried and proven M61A1 Vulcan with 570 rounds of ammunition. Its six revolving barrels give a rate of fire of 100 rounds-per-second combined with a muzzle velocity of 3,400ft(1,036m)/sec, using M50 series ammunition. Firing the M61 causes a high level of vibration, and in both the F-15 and F-16 it is mounted in the starboard wing root to keep it away from the sensitive electronics of the radar, countering the eccentric loads imposed by the recoil by calling up a touch of rudder when the gun is fired. In the Hornet, this was not possible because the gun would have spoiled the sensitive aerodynamics of

the LERX, and so the M61 is located on the optimum centreline position, just behind the radar, with the gunport just above the nose. Clever damping was used to reduce the vibration to acceptable levels. At one time it was thought that this might cause problems as the sticky gun exhaust gas would blow back over the windshield and blur the forward view, but firing trials showed that there was no problem. Nor were problems encountered in night-firing trials, even though the muzzle flash is just ahead of the pilot.

The AIM-9L Sidewinder and the

AIM-7M Sparrow are the two main air-to-air missiles.

The Sidewinder is essentially a visual distance, close-combat weapon, with a Vmax of 2.5, a static range of 10nm (19km) at high altitude reducing to about one third of this distance at low-level, and a seeker "look" angle wide enough to enable it to track manoeuvring targets. It homes in on the heat emissions of the target, either the engine exhaust plume, or "hot spots" on the airframe, which allows it to be launched from any angle. Its main faults are an inability to see

Above: The ninth single seat FSD Hornet was the first to receive the air superiority grey finish.

Below: An inert Sparrow is punched clear during early weapons separation trials.

Below: A VMFA-314 Black Knight's F/A-18A launches a Sidewinder from the right rail.

through cloud or heavy rain, and a tendency to be fooled by decoy flares.

The Sparrow is a medium-range missile with a Vmax of Mach 3.7 and a static range of 54nm (10km) at high altitude reducing significantly at low level. While it can be launched at a target from any angle, it performs best from head-on at high closing speeds. It gives the Hornet a genuine beyond visual range (BVR) kill capability, always supposing that the target can be positively identified as hostile. It homes on the reflected radar emissions of the launching fighter, which therefore has to illuminate the target during the entire time of flight of the missile. This is not a good thing, as it makes the launching fighter too predictable, while also forcing it to

Above: A test fire of an AIM-7 Sparrow over the Pacific Missile Test range at Point Mugu.

Left: In this test firing of a live Sparrow, the missile does not appear to separate cleanly.

continue closing in on the enemy. Other faults are that the radar emissions can warn the target of impending attack, while the sensitivity of the seeker head tends to curtail severely the range at which a target with low radar reflectivity can be attacked to well within the dynamic limits of the missile. Finally, only one target can be engaged at a time.

The AIM-120A AMRAAM has been developed to replace the Sparrow

Above: The Hornet is cleared to use AGM-65 Maverick, the USN version of which is at the rear.

Vmax is about Mach 5, and static range at high altitude is roughly 40nm (74km). The target is detected and a predicted position is fed to the missile's electrons. The missile is then launched, giving no indications to the target that it is on its way. At intervals it receives course updates from its parent fighter; then when the predicted range has closed down to about 10nm (19km) or less, it switches on its active radar and completes the interception with no further outside help. To a great degree it is a "fire-and-forget" weapon, which is to its advantage, and it also allows the Hornet to engage multiple targets simultaneously, mid-course updates for the missiles being done on a timeshare basis. Its main disadvantage is its high cost.

In the fighter role, the Hornet carries two Sparrows on the fuselage corner conformal stations, and two Sidewinders on wingtip rails. The outboard underwing points carry either two Sidewinders each, for a total of eight missiles, or one Sparrow each for a total of six. In the attack role, the two wingtip Sidewinders are carried to give a credible self-defence capability.

The Hornet is also cleared to carry three types of air-to-surface missiles; the AGM-65E/F Maverick, AGM-88A High-Speed Anti-Radiation Missile (HARM), and the AGM-84 Harpoon.

Above: In the anti-shipping role the Hornet can carry two AGM-84A Harpoon missiles.

The first of these comes in two versions; the laser-guided AGM-65E used by USMC Hornets for precision attacks against hard targets, and the IIR AGM-65F for USN use against shipping and coastal objectives. Both are relatively short-ranged weapons which rely on visual or electro-optical target acquisition before launch. HARM is a short range anti-radiation missile used for defence-suppression, which homes onto the emissions of enemy ground radars. Both Maverick and HARM are rocket-propelled. Harpoon is, by contrast, a medium-range, anti-shipping, sea-skimming

Avionics and Armament

Above: While the Hornet can carry ordnance on triple or multiple ejector racks, the twin, seen here, is the standard fit.

Top: ''Bombs away'', as FSD Hornet No 4 salvoes nine 500lb (227kg) Mk 82 slicks. Close look reveals the recording cameras.

Above: A two seater Hornet of the Candian Armed Forces releases BL 755 CBUs over the bombing range.

missile propelled by a small turbojet. After launch it flies a preprogrammed course before switching on its active radar seeker for the terminal homing phase. As it closes in on the target, it pops up to a few hundred feet before making a diving final attack. A total of four Mavericks, HARMS, or Harpoons can be carried, one on each underwing pylon.

In addition to air-to-surface missiles, the Hornet is cleared to carry the usual types of ''smart'' bombs. These include the Paveway series of laser-guided bombs (LGB), and the now rather elderly AGM-62 Walleye. Walleye is a glide bomb with a television camera in the nose. After launch it transmits a picture via a special data link pod, back to the Hornet pilot, who locks it onto the target by electro-optical means. One Walleye can be carried on each of the outboard under-

wing pylons, the data link pod being carried on the centreline.

The "iron" weapons carried by the Hornet are pretty much a standard mix; high- and low-drag bombs, Snakeye retarded bombs, and Rockeye BL-755 cluster bomb units. Rocket launch pods can also be carried, but these would only be used against targets such as landing craft. The Canadian Armed Forces have cleared the long range unguided CRV-7 for

Above: Eight cluster bombs carried in pairs on twin ejector racks is a typical ordnance load in the close air support mission.

use by their Hornets. While in theory a Hornet can carry a total of nineteen Mk 82 500lb (227kg), this would involve the use of multiple ejector racks. The drag of these plus the weapons is unacceptably high, and twin ejector racks are commonly used, giving a more typical load of eight Mk 82s, or four Mk 84 2,000lb (907kg) bombs, plus a fuel tank on the centreline. If longer range is required, fuel tanks can also be carried on the two inboard wing pylons, albeit at the expense of ordnance. In wartime the issue is not the aircraft's load but the ability to place ordnance accurately on target and return, in spite of all the attempts of the defenders to prevent it. In this, the Hornet excels.

FROM THE outset, the Hornet was designed to replace two very different aircraft: the F-4 Phantom II and the A-7 Corsair II. The former was originally a fleet defence interceptor; but military needs dictated that it also be used in the air superiority, fighter escort, attack, reconnaissance, and defence-suppression roles. By contrast, the latter was a dedicated light attack machine that could only operate effectively in daylight and good visibility, although its accuracy of weapon delivery under these conditions became a byword.

The need to replace two so very dissimilar aircraft with a single type was dictated by the limited space aboard an aircraft carrier, the typical complement of which would be two squadrons of fighters, two light attack squadrons and one all-weather attack squadron, plus the usual force multipliers. One of the cardinal rules of warfare is security of base, and however much power a carrier can project through its attack squadrons, the first priority is always defence. In a low-threat area, the total of 24 fighters is adequate. In a high-threat area, it is simply insufficient. Not only must one or more Combat Air Patrols (CAP) be maintained around the clock, making heavy demands on both men and machines, but in the event of a strike force being launched, escort fighters would have to be provided to cover it. With a maximum effort *Alpha* strike, even a force of three carriers would be hard-pressed to put up enough fighters to provide an adequate escort while ensuring security of base.

The standard USN carrier fighter is the F-14 Tomcat. This has an unparalleled long-range interception capability, and it is also more than capable in the close-combat arena. While the large interceptors hold the outer ring of the defences, Hornets configured for air-to-air operations can operate at medium-range from the carrier. This has two advantages. Firstly, it frees the Tomcats to roam further out in search of targets before they can release their long range anti-ship missiles. Secondly, it provides defence in depth and in greater numbers. What used to be two light attack squadrons in the carrier complement becomes two extra squadrons of defending fighters. While the Hornet cannot match the long-range interception and kill capability of the Tomcat, nor its Mach 2+ dash speed, its radar and avionics suite outmatch those of any known potential adversary aircraft. As the fight closes to visual range, the Hornet becomes a more formidable adversary than even its large stablemate. Its rate of turn is only marginally less than that of the F-16; its rate of roll is now a snappy 220deg/sec, while its pitch rate is described as phenomenal. These attributes, added to its high AoA

Below: Hornets aboard CVN69 USS *Dwight D. Eisenhower*, the carrier that Randy Causey flew the millionth hour from.

capability, make it a very formidable opponent in close combat, and with its new and more powerful -402 engine, it will be even more so.

TWO PLANES IN ONE

In the attack role, the Hornet has drawn some flak because it is unable to haul quite so much ordnance quite so far as the A-7. This criticism is meaningless. The Hornet's speed, its agility, and its advanced nav/attack and countermeasures fit make it far more likely to reach the target, attack, and return unscathed, than its predecessor. It is far more survivable in a hostile environment, especially when enemy fighters are about. In a low-threat environment it can operate without orthodox fighter escort. It can fight after a fashion with a heavy load on, although this is not recommended, and would only be used to negate an enemy fighter attack for long enough to allow the Hornet force to slip past. But after it has dropped its load it becomes a fighter for the return trip, with two 'winders and a gun.

It is always possible to configure a proportion of the Hornet force for air-to-air to cover the attackers, but as this would reduce the amount of munitions carried, and with it the damage potential, this would only be done when the threat level made fighter escort absolutely essential, but when no Tomcats were available for the task.

ONE MILLION HOURS

When assssessing the respective strengths of two opposing forces, numerical strength can be very misleading. An aircraft on the ground is just another target; it only counters

Above: Fuelling on a crowded deck as Hornets of VMFA-314 Black Knights prepare to launch from the USS *Constellation*.

Above: Fuelling over, a Black Knights Hornet is "fed to the cat" ready for launch, while a second Hornet stands ready.

when it is in the air. In this respect the Hornet is supreme. It was designed to be in the air, not on the ground for repair or maintenance, and in this aspect it outstrips all other USN tactical fighters. There are several commonly used measures of reliability and maintainability. These are: Mean Flying Hours Between Failures (MFHBF), and Maintenenace Man Hours per Flight Hour (MMH/FH). Figures released for the whole of 1989 show that USN Hornets "spring a leak" every 1.9 hours on average. If this seems pretty disastrous, consider that other MFHBFs are 0.8 for the A-7E, 0.6 for the A-6E, and 0.5 for the F-14A! These figures are mirrored in the maintainability data. The F-14A needs 63.8 MMH/FH, the A-6E 57 hours, the A-7E 43.5 hours, while the F/A-18 figure is just 27.6 hours. In part these figures are a measure of the hostile flight environment of carrier aircraft. This is highlighted by the USMC figures. The Marines some-

times go to sea on carriers, but are more often land based. USMC F/A-18 figures for the same period are MFHBF 3.4 hours; MMH/FH 17.9 hours. Very impressive.

Statistics also show that the Hornet is the safest tactical carrier aircraft in USN history. In its first half million flight hours, attrition was just 22 aircraft. This compares well with 50 for the Tomcat, 63 for the Intruder, 95 for the Phantom II, 111 for the Corsair II, and an incredible 144 for the Skyhawk. Avionics are of course part of the story, but docile handling accounts for much of the rest.

Due to enter service in 1994 is the reconnaissance Hornet, which will replace the RF-4B in the USMC inventory. The recce pack will displace the gun, but it will be interesting to see whether the wingtip Sidewinders are retained during the mission. The standard aircraft flies better with them on, and if they are kept, the old reconnaissance motto of "Alone, Unarmed, and Unafraid" will go out of the window. This is no bad thing; it never was more than two out of the three anyway.

A measure of the Hornet's versatility

is given by the fact that it is to replace two further aircraft in the USMC inventory. These are the Douglas OA-4M Skyhawk II, and the A-6E Intruder. The Skyhawk is a fast-mover FAC, and its task is to quarter the battle area to identify targets, then call in an air strike to hit them. The Intruder is an all-weather medium-attack aircraft, and the two-seater F/A-18D will replace this, although not in the deep interdiction role.

The Hornet is now a mature weapon system, and on 10 April 1990, its millionth flight hour was recorded by Lt. Cdr. Randy Causey, USN, of VFA-136 *Knighthawks*, flying from the USS *Eisenhower* in the Mediterranean. Hardly coincidentally, it was Causey's 1,000th flight hour on type. The Hornet had achieved operational capability just seven years earlier. This rapid building of flying time is a reflection on two things: numbers and serviceability. It is going to be around for a long time yet!

THE first service units to operate the Hornet received their initial aircraft virtually simultaneously in 1981. They were the test and evaluation squadrons VX-4 *Evaluators* based at Naval Air Station (NAS) Point Mugu and VX-5 *Vampires* at Naval Weapons Center (NWC) China Lake, and the Fleet Readiness Squadron VFA-125 *Rough Raiders* at NAS Lemoore, all in California. While the job of the test outfits was exactly what one would expect, examining the operational capabilities of the Hornet in great detail, the *Rough Raiders* were tasked with preparing a training and conversion syllabus for both pilots and ground crew. Later of course they would become just one of three training outfits converting F-4 and A-7 squadrons onto the new type, and providing replacement pilots for existing Hornet squadrons, but first they had to write the ''rule book'' from scratch.

This was a unique demand. The Hornet had been designed from the outset as a multi-role fighter, and this was reflected in the original command structure. The first commander was Capt. James W. Partington, a naval officer with a store of experience in the attack mission. His executive officer was Lt. Col. Gary R. VanGysel, an experienced USMC F-4 driver. One of the main problems to be tackled was getting to grips with the advanced cockpit, which needed a great deal of manual dexterity to operate efficiently. Commissioned on 13 November 1980, by August of the following year they were ready to start air combat manoeuvring, despite having only three Hornets at this stage to be shared between 16 pilots.

The pilot training syllabus evolved by VFA-125 lasts five months and that for ground personnel a little less. It consists of four phases: conversion onto type; air-to-air; air-to-surface; and

Below: This Hornet of evaluation squadron VX-5 Vampires, based at Point Mugu, carries a ''Black Bunny'' logo on its drop tank.

carrier qualification. The first operational Hornet squadron was VMFA-314, who reached initial capability on 7 January 1983. They were followed in quick succession by their sister squadrons in Marine Air Wing 3, namely VMFA-323 and VMFA-531. The first USN squadron was not far behind, VFA-113 becoming operational in August of that year.

Although many politicians and other outsiders were critical of the Hornet, it was noticeable that no static was coming from within the cockpit. Ex-Phantom II drivers were generally ecstatic about its ease of handling and agility, while ex-Corsair men were enthusiastic about their new found ability to defend themselves without having to rely on fighter escort. Both were dazzled by the capabilities of the avionic systems and the new cockpit.

The only doubtful note, which still exists today, is whether one man can really handle the workload, making the most efficient use of all the sophisticated systems available while keeping his eyes locked on a target. While the crew station was designed to reduce pilot workload, the simplicity of the basic functions allowed a whole range of other modes to be added. Using for example the level of technology of the Phantom II, it is certain that one man could not possibly cope. The Hornet enables him to do so, but the level of concentration required is still very high, especially at night, and it is not unknown for a pilot to ''max out'' occasionally. This is one of the reasons that the USMC have gone for a dedicated two-seater for the night attack mission.

Another aspect which caused some disquiet is the fact that different men tend to be good at different things.

Right: The NJ tailcode denotes VFA-125, the Pacific Coast Fleet Readiness squadron.

Using cricket as an analogy, some specialize in batting; others in bowling. Very few are good all-rounders. By the same token, flyers tend to specialize in air combat or in ground attack. Yet the Hornet concept demands that they be good at both. This conflict has been partially resolved by allowing Hornet squadrons to have primary and secondary roles. Some concentrate on air combat; others on the attack mission. The flexibility of the aircraft allows roles to be changed at need.

FOREIGN USERS

While the USN and USMC were gradually building up their Hornet force, many other countries were looking to upgrade their own capability. Air defence was the primary scenario, but an all-rounder with a credible strike capability was very attractive. As in all things, compromise was the order of the day; a combination of

Below: Fire and noise as a CAF two seater ripples four pods of CRV-7 unguided rockets.

Above: Not a four seater multi-winged aircraft, but a perfect formation by the Blue Angels.

what they wanted and what they could afford. Often the two American giants, the F-14 Tomcat and the F-15 Eagle, were considered in the early stages, but eliminated on cost grounds. The competition therefore often devolved into a contest between the Hornet and its old adversary, the F-16 Fighting Falcon.

On purely cost grounds, the F-16 had a clear advantage, and in close combat it was marginally the better

In Service and at War

Above: One of the two-seater trainers acquired by the Royal Australian Air Force's order for 75 Hornets.

fighter. However, the Hornet had a far superior weapons system, with BVR missiles and a genuine adverse weather capability. It was more versatile, two engines gave a greater safety margin, and its survivability was arguably better. While a significant number of nations chose the F-16, where the requirements were more stringent, the F/A-18 ran out the winner.

Below: Canadian Hornets carry a painted cockpit canopy on the underside for aspect deception.

The first export customer for the Hornet was Canada, which plaed a substantial order in the summer of 1980. Two key factors were cited in their decision. Canada is an extremely large country, and airfields capable of taking fast jets are few and far between. A pilot forced to eject could be just as easily lost in the vast frozen wastes as he could when ejecting over the sea. Twin-engined safety was the main factor on which the decision turned; the other was that the Canadian Armed Forces (CAF) felt that the Hornet had better growth potential.

The Canadian Hornet was designated CF-18, and it varied from the USN version in a number of relatively minor ways. Recessed into the left side of the forward fuselage is a 600,000-candlepower spotlight. This is a standard CAF item used for the visual identification of possible "bogeys" at night. The USN automatic carrier landing system (ACLS) was replaced by an instrument landing system (ILS), and a cold weather overland survival pack carried in lieu of the USN sea survival gear.

Finally, the CF-18 has a dummy canopy painted on its underside in matt black. The purpose of this is to provide a measure of aspect deception in close combat. Opinons as to its efficacy differ. Some nations regard it as a hazard in peacetime air combat manoeuvring, while at a more personal level American Aggressor pilot Major Joe Hodges states categorically that if you are close enough to see it you are too close to be fooled!

Initially, attrition in CAF service was lower than expected, which caused the CAF not to take up its option for a follow-on batch of Hornets. More recently there has been a spate of crashes, and concern has been expressed that the information explosion in the cockpit to which the Hornet pilot is subjected, combined with the agility of the aircraft, may cause the pilot to become disorientated. As a result, training in basic flying has been intensified, while afterburner take-offs at night, and the use of afterburner during instrument flight conditions, has been restricted.

Below: Canadian fighter pilots are proud of their Hornets, and advertise the fact by wearing this shoulder patch.

The next export customer was Australia. Like Canada, the Royal Australian Air Force (RAAF) has a large and inhospitable country to defend, while much of their flying is done over water, and maritime surveillance is one of their top priorities. Again, selection devolved into a head-to-head contest with the F-16. The choice was made on three counts. These were twin-engined safety, better growth potential, and superior avionics. Australian Hornets differ slightly from the standard article. They do not carry catapult launch equipment, the ACLS is replaced by a conventional ILS, and they carry a high-frequency radio for long-distance communications. In addition they have indigenous TACAN, IFF, and fatigue monitoring systems, an aural gear down warning system, and a landing light.

While most RAAF Hornets were licence-built, the first two were delivered from the USA. This involved a non-stop flight to RAAF Williamtown from NAS Lemoore in California of 6,672nm (12,364km), accompanied by a USAF KC-10 Extender for in-flight refuelling. Lasting 15 hours, this broke the previous fighter endurance record of 11 hours which had been set by British Harriers

in 1982, and it did so by a healthy margin. A total of thirteen refuellings were made in order to keep the Hornets fully topped up in case of an emergency.

The third export operator of the Hornet was Spain. The Ejercito del Aire needed an all-weather, multi-role fighter to replace its F-4C Phantom IIs, Mirages and F-5As. Once again, the main opposition was the F-16, and the superior avionics system of the Hornet won the day. Spanish Hornets

Below: South Korea is currently having doubts about its proposed purchase of Hornets.

Above: Spain's Ejercito del Aire chose the F/A-18 to replace its ageing F-4s, Mirages, and F-5As, rather than the F-16.

are designated EF-18s, E standing for Espana.

In more recent times, three further nations have announced that they are placing orders for the Hornet. Switzerland stated that its choice was influenced by the docile handling characteristics and the superior radar/avionics suite of the Hornet, which made it more suitable for use in mountainous terrain. In mid-1990 they announced that they were to re-evaluate the contenders, and until this is done the Swiss order is on the backburner. Kuwait ordered 40 Hornets, and despite rumours to the contary and events during the Gulf War, this order still stands. For it to have been cancelled would have been to admit that Iraq permanently possessed the country. In December 1989, South Korea announced that it had selected the Hornet, the reasons stated being that it has the ability to counter North Korea's latest aircraft (the MiG-29 Fulcrum); that they had to operate the aircraft for 30 years; geographical considerations like mountainous terrain

In Service and at War

and the sea on three sides made the Hornet more suitable, and that the Hornet possessed greater capability than its competitors.

LIBYA AND KUWAIT

The Hornet has proved its worth in the crucible of war. The first occasion was in 1986 against Libya; a time when Libyan leader Colonel Ghaddaffy was claiming the Gulf of Sidra as Libyan territorial waters. The US Sixth Fleet was soon embroiled, and the USS *Coral Sea,* one of two American aircraft carriers to embark four squadrons of Hornets instead of two squadrons of Tomcats and two of Hornets (the other is the USS *Midway*) found itself in the thick of the action. Hornets of VFA-131 and 132, and VMFA-314 and 323 played a part in the sinking of several Libyan patrol boats in Operation *"Prairie Fire".*

This was followed a short while later by Operation *"Eldorado Canyon"*, the bombing of military targets on the Libyan mainland, in which the same units took part, flying CAP and defence suppression missions in which they used HARM missiles.

This was followed almost five years later by Operation *"Desert Storm"*; the huge air action mounted against Iraq in the first quarter of 1991 to free Kuwait from Iraqi occupation. Roughly 184 Hornets, of which 38 were F/A-18C/Ds, took part, comprising 15 squadrons. At sea, USN units VFA-15, 25, 33, 81, 83, 87, 113, 151, 192 and 195 were deployed on five carriers. On land, USMC squadrons VMFA-235, 314, 333 and 451 were based at Al Maharraq AB in Bahrein, while No 409 Squadron of the Canadian Armed Forces operated out of Dohar AB in Qatar.

Most of their work consisted of attacks on Iraqi ground forces, and a few strikes were made against Iraqi naval units, but some counter-air missions were also flown. On the second day of the war, F/A-18C Hornets from the USS *Saratoga* encountered Iraqi fighters, shooting down two MiG-29 Fulcrums. This engagement was probably the baptism of fire in air combat for both types, and success against Soviet-built fighters highly regarded in the West was very encouraging.

Above: Hornets of VMFA-314 have been engaged in action against both Libya and Iraq.

Below: An eight-strong "swarm" of Hornets from VFA-131 operating from USS Coral Sea.

Below: With wings folded, Hornets take up minimal deck space on a carrier.

Further aerial victories may have been scored by Hornets; in all some 20 Iraqi aircraft known to have been downed in air combat remain unattributed at the time of writing.

The operation was not, however, conducted without loss. On the first day of the war an F/A-18C from VFA-81, flying from the USS *Saratoga*, was downed by a SAM, while a second Hornet from an unidentified unit went missing on 7 February while returning to its carrier.

The sole Canadian squadron was mainly employed in air defence operations. Late in the war it was announced that they would commence flying attack missions after a brief period of retraining, but the war ended before this was completed.

The early days of the Hornet were often blighted by those who sought its cancellation, often on the flimsiest of pretexts. Its service career, now crowned by outstanding war service in the skies of Kuwait and Iraq, has proved them specatcularly wrong.

Below: Hornet handling is very docile, as demonstrated by this lineup in the Gulf.

Above: A close formation of factory fresh Hornets of VFA-15 Valions, with wingtip winders.

Below: A retractable probe is used for inflight refuelling, using a towed drogue receptacle.

INDEX